$ECRETS OF A SUCCESSFUL GOLD BUYER

How to Buy & Sell Gold & Silver Jewelry, Coins & Bullion as an Entrepreneur, Investor, Collector, Or Fundraiser

METAL MAN

Be A Gold Buyer, Intl.

ISBN: 978-0-615-45608-9

Library of Congress Control Number: 2011903964

Library of Congress Subject headings:
Gold—Purchasing
New business enterprises—Management
Metals as an investment
Precious metals—Handbooks, manuals, etc.

Proudly printed in The United States of America

CONTENTS

ACKNOWLEDGEMENTS

Metal Man works hard but has been helped. Here is my chance to specially recognize the valuable contributions of others. To all those listed: please accept my heartfelt thanks.

Thank you, my better half, for your support and encouragement. Words fail me to describe this true treasure by my side. You are and ever will be worth more to me than all the gold in the world.

Thank you, CEO and Love Bug, for blessing me every day even just by your presence. I hope that, long before you ever read this, you already know how cherished you are. By the way, CEO, your handsome little face added personality to my website.

Thank you, T., for your generosity in the beginning. I don't forget it.

Thank you, B., for sharing your knowledge. Those questions would have gone unanswered but for you.

Thank you, Metal Man customers and book buyers, for allowing me the privilege to serve you.

Thank You, most of all, my beloved God and Savior, for redemption, direction, provision, and protection. Please work through this book to the benefit of others, and may You get all the credit.

INTRODUCTION

You are about to enter the clandestine world of gold buyers. Picture a *Mission Impossible* movie—sans the imminent danger and international espionage. Gold buyers' tactical maneuvers involve all kinds of clever devices and confidential techniques. They work out in the open but reveal few clues about their entrepreneurial operations. Their insider secrets, long hidden from the public, afford them a lucrative livelihood.

As a prospective gold buyer, my search for information yielded little. I found and purchased a homemade booklet online. The author touted it as a tell-all. Instead, it gave a general overview of gold buying and lacked depth. Either he retained key details or didn't know them. The booklet should have taught me the lessons in advance that I later learned the hard way.

It was better than nothing but not nearly as good as it could have been. However, I turned my hurdle into your springboard. Now there is a comprehensive resource available to you: this book. These pages reveal the secrets of successful gold buying.

Most business owners would *never* tell you their proprietary secrets. Sharing secrets would be giving away what they worked hard to attain. Ask Famous Amos for his cookie recipe or Calvin Klein for his cologne ingredients. Try persuading an eBay Powerseller to name just one true, useful wholesaler. You'll get nothing.

Gold buyers are no different. Some offer select tidbits as a marketing strategy. They share no more than necessary to win trust and, consequently, customers. A few even offer to "train" potential buyers. They tell just enough to recruit agents and/or charge a hefty fee. Therefore, even the fundamentals are elusive—let alone all the useful tips that savvy professionals know. Similarly, as a successful gold buyer I rarely divulged any secrets.

Fortunately for you, that time is past; I am no longer an active gold buyer. I left my successful business to pursue personal interests. As an ex-gold buyer there is no need for me to remain tight-lipped. In fact, it behooves me now as an author to share everything I know with my readers. Such is the purpose of this book.

Secrets of a Successful Gold Buyer explains the logistics of buying and selling precious metals for profit. It also illustrates my business model. You don't have to replicate it, though. You can set up a sole proprietorship or a corporation. You can start off mobile, rent an office or lease a storefront. You can buy from the public or other gold buyers, or both. You can fill your workday with appointments or work exclusively through gold parties. Personalize my strategy to fit your particular situation. The information in this book will equip you for any gold buying future.

I write from a business perspective, because that was my experience. Indeed gold buying can be a lucrative career path. Still, not all gold buyers are motivated by professional pursuit. Gold buying is also a solid investment plan, a rewarding hobby, and an easy fundraiser.

Common investors purchase gold for their portfolios, paying *full price plus* assorted fees. They hope for big gains to make their money back. You will learn how to amass unlimited amounts at a fraction of market value. That way, you shrewdly secure your profit when you buy. Furthermore, common market fluctuations won't send you into the red.

Most hobbies absorb money; gold buying can generate money. Hungry collectors gobble up gold and silver coins and bullion at premium prices. Like the investor, you will be able to acquire them below market value. That helps you enjoy them without fretting the cost. Later, you can liquidate individual pieces or parts of your collection without paying a dealer's commission.

Forget about selling buttons or cupcakes to raise needed funds for your organization. Solicit donations of unwanted jewelry. Then sell it to the companies listed in this book, rather than a gold buyer, at almost full value. You can even purchase it from your contributors; both parties will benefit. A "gold drive" requires far less organization and hoopla than charity auctions or selling $100 bricks for a new building. Gold offers a wonderfully simple, lucrative alternative.

I wrote *Secrets of a Successful Gold Buyer* for gold buyers of all kinds. It is the first comprehensive guide ever published for active and aspiring buyers, full-time and part-time, in all English-speaking countries. It contains sound advice and proven techniques for entrepreneurs, investors, collectors, and fundraisers. Its thorough chapters explain *everything* I learned as a successful gold buyer. Numerous examples, tables, figures, lists, footnotes, and appendices all supplement the instruction.

If experience is the best teacher, let me teach you from my experience. You can avoid the trial and error method by which I was forced to learn. Furthermore, you can start where I ended—miles ahead of the novice and in the company of seasoned professionals. Your success is my aim; read on.

CHAPTER 1

PRIMARY BRIEFING: GOLD BUYER BASICS

Basic Questions

What is a Gold Buyer?

A gold buyer purchases precious metal items below market value and resells them for a profit. He buys from, and resells to, individuals and businesses. Most gold buyers are full-time professionals. Yet savvy investors, collectors, and fundraisers can benefit as gold buyers too. Gold buyers are also called "precious metal buyers" and "scrappers".

As you may have deduced already, gold buyers buy gold. Most buy silver too. Some purchase platinum, palladium, and even diamonds. This book specifically addresses gold and silver. However, readers can apply the information to other metals as well.

Gold Buyers can make a lot of money with a little work. They also can evolve with changing trends and diversify to expand. I was a successful gold buyer; this book explains how you can be too.

Why Become a Gold Buyer?

Gold buying is an outstanding business opportunity. How can I claim it rivals the best money making ideas, though? The media is crowded with people promoting ways to make money. Realistically, many strategies won't work for most people. Furthermore, few *proven* methods can match the benefits and potential of gold buying. Yet you want facts—not hyperbole. So here are 5 excellent reasons why you should become a gold buyer now:

- ★ Successful gold buyers get rich!
- ★ Gold buyers are in demand!
- ★ You can begin making big money with a small investment!
- ★ This business is easy to learn!
- ★ Gold buyers can set their own schedules!

Buying and selling gold and silver can be enormously profitable. This business offers a normal profit margin; nevertheless, gold buyers deal in high dollar amounts. That modest margin translates into substantial income. Regularly, single transactions can yield hundreds of dollars in profits. *Frequently,* you can net thousands in a day.

This business boasts built-in demand. Gold is ubiquitous, and so are customers. people everywhere are looking to sell their scrap jewelry, inheritances, and late husbands' coin collections. They seek a buyer for their gold and silver jewelry, bullion, and silverware. They need quick cash or just want to liquidate their items. The successful gold buyer simply positions himself in front of the clamoring crowd. You can be this gold buyer.

The business of gold buying can be a shoestring startup.[$] It's cheap, like the adult version of a lemonade stand (except entirely more profitable). The start-up costs are exceptionally low if you compare costs to earnings potential. This activity requires only a few inexpensive tools and some cash on hand. You *can* launch into gold buying for under a thousand dollars; two or three thousand ensures an easier entry.

You need not be a rocket scientist or even a college graduate to buy gold. My book offers clear and thorough directions; just follow them. The technical aspects are routine and unchanging, so there is a sharp learning curve. First, memorize the basic details and standard procedure. Then coast. The only foreseeable changes would be those you institute in your marketing.

Gold buyers make money by providing a service; you must be available to clients. You can choose your hours and select your workdays, though. When you work from home

---

[$] Generally, the term "shoestring" is applied to businesses which require less than $5000 to set up.

you can take a day off. With a home business you can "open" at noon if you like. Making money doesn't have to mean working to exhaustion. Buy gold part-time or full-time. Work 4–12 hours per day, 3–7 days per week. Family, friends, and outside interests are important. Establish your own balance between work and leisure.

Is There a Catch?

One problem has prevented many would-be gold buyers from entering the industry. The same obstacle has held back some current buyers from higher success. The problem: successful gold buyers guard their secrets. Their secrecy deters upstarts and helps them retain the upper hand over competition.

Gold buying is an insider business—the kind that stays in families. Fathers pass it on to their kids who pass it on to their kids. A hopeful gold buyer needs a willing and knowledgeable teacher. Otherwise, confusion and folly will sabotage his efforts.

Now, however, this is no longer a problem. Finally, an experienced gold buyer discloses his insider information. This groundbreaking guide, *Secrets of a Successful Gold Buyer,* gives you an unprecedented opportunity.

Basic Materials

Gold and Silver

Most gold and silver items are composed of precious metal alloys; they are *not* 100% pure. The various alloys contain different concentrations of gold or silver, as shown in the tables below. We refer to each alloy according to its purity. However, we commonly express silver purities in decimal form but refer to karat values of gold.

GOLD ALLOYS

Alloy	Purity
6K	.25
7K	.291
8K	.333
9K	.375
10K	.4166
12K	.500
14K	.583
18K	.750
22K	.9166
24K	.999

Table 1.1

SILVER ALLOYS

Alloy	Purity
800	.800
Coin Silver	.900
Sterling	.925
Bullion	.999

Table 1.2

Gold

Classic gold is yellow. However, white and rose (or pink) are other common colors. Lime color is seen less often, and exotic varieties exist but are rare. The different colors are created by altering the proportions of the other metals in the alloy. These can include copper, nickel, zinc, manganese, silver, palladium, platinum, and rhodium coating.

Some items are composed of multiple gold colors. Professionals refer to these as two-tone, three-tone or multi-color. For instance, most Black Hills Gold pieces can be labeled as two-tone (yellow and rose gold) or three-tone (with white gold). Incidentally, green gold replaces one of these varieties in some pieces.

Gold purities range from 6–24K. Though common in the UK, anything less than 10K gold is rare in the US. Many of these pieces arrive here on travelers, as personal items; they are not widely sold in the states. Fine 22K and 24K gold from South Korea, Saudi Arabia, and other countries are more common. Due to rarity and demand they are perfect for reselling rather than refining. Overall, the most prevalent US varieties are 10K, 14K, and 18K gold.

Divide the karat value by 24 to find the decimal value for a gold variety (Table 1.1). For example, divide 14K by 24 (since there are 24 karats in pure gold). Following the math, a 14K gold item contains a .583 concentration of gold. In other words, 14K gold is 58.3% pure, or “fine”. Later you will use these decimals to calculate the value of items.

Different karat items may all look nearly the same to an average consumer and a fledgling gold buyer. Yet experienced buyers can distinguish each from the other. The gold color is deeper and richer in higher karat items. Pure 24K gold exhibits a unique luster that 8K gold barely resembles.

Gold plated and gold filled items consist of a base metal covered by a gold layer. Usually, "gold filled" indicates gold on copper composition. (Incidentally, most 12K gold is gold filled.) Steel, nickel, copper, and brass are the common base metals in gold plated items. Mainly, the difference between the two categories is the production process. The commodity value of any of these pieces ranges from nil to nominal.

Gold plated silver is called "vermeil" (Ver-MAY). It is yellow like gold but stamped "925" to indicate sterling. To you it is worth the same as any other sterling and only for assay.[$] You can assay vermeil with sterling. However, a refinery will not purchase it outright with a load of sterling.[$]

Silver

Silver, a white-grey colored metal, is far less valuable than gold. Ironically, though, most gold alloys are more diluted than silver alloys. The sterling standard requires 92.5% (.925) silver content. Common coin silver, at 90% fine, is only slightly less pure. Even the 800 silver (.800)

[$] Assay explanation begins on page 50.
[$] Refineries explained in Chapter 4.

found in European silverware and jewelry is more pure than 18K gold. Generally, copper comprises the other part of silver alloys.

Table 1.2 lists four types of silver. These varieties account for the vast majority of silver items. However, old silverware does not always follow this rule. In some cases it was made from unusual silver alloys, though usually stamped with a number (and/or a hallmark). The stamped number indicates the purity, but hallmarks require research.

Fine silver has a moonlike glow to it. I am not trying to be fancy; that is just the best way to describe silver. The glow can be particularly noticeable in large pieces. In contrast, plated and steel items look like shiny chrome. Unlike gold, silver oxidizes or tarnishes over time.

Silver sets (flatware and tea sets) are notoriously silver plated. Many clients insist their silverware is sterling just because it is old. Age does *not* establish purity! Companies have been silver plating since 1857 when the process was first applied to jewelry. Eventually you will probably recognize most silver plated sets right away.

Bullion and Coins

Bullion

"Bullion" is a general term. It denotes pure (.999) or nearly pure gold or silver coins, rounds, ingots, and bars. Coins and rounds are round. Basically, coins weigh 1 ozt or less and are federally contracted.[$] Rounds are 1 ozt in size, or bigger, and privately minted. Ingots and bars are both rectangular and their distinctions are inexact. Ingots weigh a few grams on up to a few troy ounces; bars are heavier. Bullion comes in numerous sizes and seemingly infinite designs.

Standard bullion bears a "999" or "999 FINE" marking (except some coins) along with its weight in grams or troy ounces. Most bars and ingots also are stamped with a serial number. Substandard bullion differs drastically.

Substandard ingots and bars look homemade. Usually these are stamped with the weight only. Its weight might even be a random weight—not a round weight. For example, it could display "9.3 ozt", instead of "10 ozt". They are stamped with an unrecognized manufacturer name—if at all.

Buyers and collectors consider these pieces less desirable or even suspicious. The items do not command the same rate as standard bullion. Some refineries will not buy them outright due to doubts about purity. Then they only accept them for assay. A successful gold buyer also pays less for these items than for standard bullion.

US gold buyers see American Gold Eagles and Silver Eagles more than any other bullion coins. They both contain 1 ozt of fine metal. Fractional size Gold Eagles are available too, including 1⁄10, 1⁄4, and 1⁄2 ozt versions. Buyers in other countries likely find their national coins are predominant.

[$] Measurements explained on page 113.

See Appendix A for specific details about common world bullion coins.

Beware of the Chinese Panda bullion coin! It is the most counterfeited coin in the entire universe. The design changes every year, and details about the different versions could fill a small book.

Short of administering an acid test, authenticity can be difficult to establish. Details on the coin should be sharp and clear—not smooth or lacking intricacy. Look for a denomination and face value designation; only the 1982 design omitted it. Appendix C lists a website where you can learn more about counterfeit panda coins.

Some bullion is privately produced. Credit Suisse and Engelhard are leading private mints. They produce basic gold and silver bars and ingots. Companies like the Hoffman Mint and Franklin Mint manufacture collector bullion. Collector bullion is characterized by surface designs in addition to the standard markings.

Collector bullion varieties are seemingly infinite. One example is a 1 ozt round featuring Garfield on its face. A 3 ozt Mickey Mantle silver baseball card replica is another. Once I bought and sold a set of 4 ozt silver $100 bill replicas. From Santa Claus to Superman, collector bullion bears it all.

Some other items are made to look like collector bullion; check markings carefully. What appears to be gold bullion might be 14K gold or gold plated instead. Some silver ingots and rounds may surprise you with a "Sterling" stamp. Search for markings and check COAs when available.[$]

Some collectible rounds and ingots feature a clear or translucent colored plastic coating. The layer may degrade over time resulting in unattractive discoloration. Additionally, certain refineries pay only sterling price for these since the layer complicates the refining process. Adjust your price accordingly.

The collector bullion category also includes silver casino tokens. It is a common misconception that casino tokens are 1 ozt rounds. Actually, only the center is .999 silver; the rim is brass. The center must be popped out of the rim before refining. Each token contains about .6 ozt pure silver. Some refineries assume a content of .5 ozt and pay accordingly.

Coins

Occasionally, a client's items will include a rare coin. With a price guide and a strategy to resell numismatics, you can profit from that situation.[$] However, only dealers seek such collectibles. The successful gold buyer focuses on junk silver (and bullion coins). Rare coins are just a beneficial byproduct.

Appendix B details common world junk silver coins. The "junk" portion of the term refers to their lack of

---

[$] New collector bullion comes with a Certificate of Authenticity.
[$] Coin price guides are explained on page 78.

numismatic value. For the most part, only their silver content determines their value. However, old silver coins in especially good condition can be worth more.

As a US buyer I rarely saw foreign junk silver. Americans who buy junk silver usually buy American junk silver. I only encountered foreign silver coins as miscellaneous items—one or two at a time. Non-U.S. buyers may see the same pattern in their own countries.

Standard pricing for junk silver is expressed as a multiple of face value. “Face value” refers to a coin’s denomination. For example, two quarters and five dimes equal $1 of face value altogether.

Let’s say your refinery buys 90% silver coins for “eight times face”. Then the aforementioned six coins would be worth $8 total (8 × $1 = $8) to them. Refineries may also quote you a rate like “$8”. This still means $8 times the total face value.

CHAPTER 2

BACKGROUND CHECK: METAL MAN'S STORY

A chronic medical condition precludes me from full-time employment. Besides that, I lack formal training. It sounds like a ticket to nowhere, doesn't it? Nonetheless, my responsibility is to support my family. These points motivated me to consider unconventional ways to generate income—to find one that could work within my circumstances.

Trying to find a legitimate moneymaking opportunity is like looking for Waldo. In this case, you're looking for a 3-inch tall Waldo on an IMAX screen-sized "Where's Waldo?" book page. On top of that, it's the page where Waldo is surrounded by a sea of look-alikes.

There are many good ideas for earning income. Moreover, there are thousands of ways to waste money and hope which only profit the pitchmen. Few authentic opportunities fit my criteria. Additionally, they were obscured by scams and empty hype. Fortuitously, I eventually found much more than I had hoped for.

I don't remember how I came across the idea of buying and selling gold. It didn't immediately strike me as the magical answer to my conundrum, though. Instead, I stumbled upon it, was intrigued, and began investigating. The only resource I could find was a homemade booklet online; so I bought it.

The booklet gave general information without divulging the best secrets. I finished it with unanswered questions but serious interest. Then I moved forward, armed with basic instruction and a handful of terms. This bit of knowledge led me to my first refinery.

As the finish line is to a runner, so the refinery is to a gold buyer. Refineries buy scrap metals from gold buyers based on current market prices. That particular refinery paid slightly less than others. On the other hand, they accepted any size load, or "assay". It was unique among refineries and facilitated my entry into gold buying.

They didn't impose a minimum *and* they paid the same rate for all size loads. Think of it like a wholesaler who doesn't require a $2000 minimum purchase for orders. Plus they offer the same wholesale price to any size buyer. That refinery was the *only* option for a shoestring startup like me.

Buying and selling gold works like the retail industry. The product transitions through several stops before reaching its final destination. Meanwhile its price increases each time it changes hands.

Think of the gold buyer as an agent between wholesalers and distributors in this chain. He buys from customers at wholesale prices and sells to a refinery just below retail prices. The refinery purifies the metal and sells it to other companies. Many of those companies produce goods from it and retail them to the public. The gold buyer makes a substantial profit for his part.

It seemed like a promising opportunity, but I needed to prove its potential. I contemplated and remembered something helpful.

Some heavy silver necklaces from my teenage years were sitting in my closet. They were the perfect test sample—large and worthless to me. Therefore, though moderately valuable, it didn't bother me to mail them away for refining. It was a chance at a new career. Furthermore, I expected it would pay *something* for my effort even if it didn't work out as hoped.

I discussed it with my better half, and we mailed my necklaces to that refinery. Around two weeks later I received a check for approximately $200. The envelope also contained a statement showing the gold content by weight and the refinery's calculations. Eureka! It was like discovering $200 in my coat pocket. The difference was that, with some work, I could do it again. . . and again. My mind filled with possibilities.

That first payoff served as seed money. It paid for an acid test kit and a calculator, receipt book, digital scale, binder, and business cards. I already owned a briefcase and, thus, needed no other equipment was needed at that point.

Starting a legal business involves jumping through certain bureaucratic hoops.[$] US entrepreneurs must first decide your business structure. A number of books address this topic thoroughly. Another step is to choose a DBA ("Doing Business As") name and register it at the city and, possibly, state levels. Buyers who resell items to the public within their home states must register to collect sales tax. Some jurisdictions may impose other requirements on gold buyers.

I organized as a sole proprietorship—the most basic structure. Liability issues didn't concern me. Therefore, forming a corporation to protect my personal assets was unnecessary. My city only required me to register my business name, Metal Man, with the Registrar's Office. That was the only regulation—just one hoop.

The city imposed other obligations on pawn shops and recyclers. Those sellers were forced to follow bothersome procedures to document and check their purchases. Fortunately, city officials excluded me from that group. It could not have been easier.

Next I posed as a customer and called other buyers. I inquired about their buy prices. Then I calculated their rates by comparing them against actual market values. Of the people I contacted, basic buyers paid 50–60% of actual value on average. Jewelers' rates tended toward the lower end of that range or less. Pawn shops and sell-by-mail

---

[$] I am unqualified to offer suggestions on business structures in other countries. Search online for information and consult government agencies.

companies (those seen on television and the internet) altogether paid far less. I intended to pay more than any of them.

I needed notes next. So I typed directions for identifying and testing metals, as well as formulas for determining value. The prepared pages went in plastic binder sleeves and then in my binder. They functioned as "cheat sheets" at which I could peek discreetly while conducting business. It was an essential aid until I memorized the routine. Even afterwards, I always carried this binder to remedy temporary memory lapses.

Metal Man was ready for business. I offered my service (example shown in Figure A) on local websites that featured free classified ads. My ads explained my service and the reasons to choose Metal Man. They emphasized the benefits of dealing with me and called customers to action. The keywords or "buzz words" they contained resonated with people; yet they were not grossly manipulative. Those ad sites reported to internet search engines like Google. As a result, my ads showed up when local people searched online for gold buyers.

Example of Metal Man Ad

> Get CA$H for your Gold & Silver! METAL MAN pays cash for your gold and silver jewelry, coins, sterling flatware, and more. We pay more and come to you. "No Hassle Guarantee". Metal Man is a proud member of the (removed city) Chamber of Commerce.[$] CALL NOW! (removed number) Must be 18 or older. No stolen property please. Photo ID required.

Figure A

High payouts and customer convenience shaped my business model. Renting a storefront or office would have reduced my profit margin. I didn't have the money for that and didn't want to sit around all day. Instead, I traveled to customers' homes and workplaces. By saving money on overhead I could afford to pay a little more than other buyers.

Many buyers succeed with shops, but my clients preferred their own familiar surroundings. Offering them the choice of location scored points for Metal Man. Additionally, clients appreciated sparing an errand from their to-do lists. Many chose Metal Man due to my flexibility to visit them almost anywhere, anytime during the day.

I remember my first call. The young lady hoped to sell a few gold pieces. She invited me to her house the next day. I was nervous, excited, and clueless about what to expect.

[$] The word "removed" replaces identifying details in all cases.

When I arrived at her door, she opened it and greeted me. I introduced myself and offered a handshake. We sat down at her dining room table where she handed me a few rings. I examined the rings and tested them to confirm purity. Meanwhile, she asked me a few questions.

I had to think quickly when she asked, “How long have you been doing this?” Obviously, she would not have been impressed to discover she was my first customer. With that in mind, I gently redirected the conversation. I summarized my situation and remarked that God had opened this door for me.

The chat was a pleasant exchange. Trading $150 for her gold rings was more than pleasant. I remember the price like it was yesterday. I arrived, a hopeful speculator; I departed, a professional gold buyer.

My phone rang a week and half later with the next customer. The second meeting differed from the first—quite an embarrassment. My scale stopped working in the middle of the appointment. The customer even gave me some batteries from her car’s glove compartment, which didn’t resolve the situation. I later discovered that the batteries in my scale had corroded slightly and affected one of the metal contacts. At the time, I was forced to *guess* the weight of her gold!

Though unprofessional, it was profitable. Moreover, it benefitted me as an early learning experience too. Some lessons will compensate you more than a transaction.

So it went. Every few days another caller wanted to sell me gold. I habitually used MapQuest.com to pinpoint addresses and print directions. Within two months I began scheduling multiple appointments per day. MapQuest also made it a cinch to plan routes for these occasions. From that $200 seed my new business sprouted and budded.

I mailed metals to the refinery after every two deals. I needed the money back quickly in order to continue buying. Refineries don't send checks immediately, though; the entire process takes about two weeks. So my funds lagged behind demand. People called when I didn't have enough money. I tried scheduling appointments several days out to ensure my liquidity.

The two-week turnaround proved too slow. I temporarily resorted to selling my lots to a bigger buyer. He bought from anyone and maintained separate rates for the public and other buyers. He paid me more than I paid sellers but less than refinery rates. I didn't like giving up some of my profit, but I needed immediate cash. In time I earned enough to bypass this hazard.

I would have profited more in the beginning by selling to a refinery. However, I couldn't afford to buy while waiting two weeks for settlement. A gold buyer *needs* a thousand dollars to get going. Nonetheless, starting with a few thousand dollars will help you avoid these pitfalls.

The following months brought about shocking advancements. That other buyer revealed his refinery to me during a casual conversation. He must have thought we both knew about it. Subsequently, that refinery became Metal Man's best friend in the business.

Gold buyers from my city had used a local refinery for a long time. The local refinery paid them a 98% rate, but had closed down recently. In order to attract their patronage, the other refinery offered a 98% rate exclusively to those buyers. That refinery assumed I was one of those buyers, since I came from the same city. Thus the refinery associate offered me a 98% rate, instead of the standard 95% rate, on my first visit.[$] The extra 3% translated into a hefty sum of money over the course of our involvement.

Meanwhile, I focused my attention on an affluent part of the city and its neighboring suburb. I joined the Chamber of Commerce in that suburb. Such a membership endowed me with unique credibility among gold buyers. Furthermore, a new friend helped me create a website. Suddenly I was the only local gold buyer with a website. Metal Man had evolved into an established business with maximum momentum.

I received numerous calls per day. Sometimes my phone rang nonstop like a pizzeria on a Friday night. People saw my ads or found my website and wanted to meet ASAP. Referrals started kicking in about that same time and played a major role in my growth. Clients wanted to sell me their metal, and I bought some big loads. They wanted to arrange gold parties; each brought $500–$2000 profit. My income was limited only by the length of my workdays.

The wind was at Metal Man's back. My business was well reputed in all the right circles, held high by a history of

---

[$] You probably won't encounter this particular situation. Yet while the details are specific to Metal Man, remarkable experiences are not. Any successful gold buyer can recount his fair share of memorable stories.

happy clients. Numerous customers called on me repeatedly, and a major portion of new customers resulted from recommendations. I had polished my presentation, streamlined my routine, and accrued priceless expertise. Barring unforeseen cataclysmic events, Metal Man's success could have continued in perpetuity.

Despite Metal Man's success I eventually left the business to follow a personal calling. Fortunately, Metal Man's end can mark your beginning. This book holds open the door of my exit as an entrance for you. Furthermore, if you walk through it, I will usher you from newbie to knowledgeable *or* from experienced to exceptional.

As a former buyer I openly share what current buyers won't reveal. Additionally, only I can offer the specific tips and strategies that secured Metal Man's standing. Therefore, the following pages divulge the secrets of a successful gold buyer.

Every job or business has *some* good days. In contrast, *most* of my days as a gold buyer were good, and *many* were amazing. Normal days padded my pockets with several hundred dollars profit. Better days bolstered my bank account by thousands.

I remember routinely meeting groups of friends with baggies full of gold. I fondly recall some customers with thousands of silver coins and stacks of Gold Eagles. In a way each transaction is like finding buried treasure. Best of all, the hunt is much easier and more predictable.

In my experience, most so-called moneymaking opportunities peddle hype. Their superlative promises set people up for big disappointments. A few individuals achieve rare success with some of them. The rest just waste their money.

Look around; you can see gold buyers everywhere. This isn't some complex, half-cocked scheme. Gold buying is a legitimate and profitable business. Guarded by insiders, the industry has remained largely inaccessible to outsiders until now.

Begin with the advantage of my know-how. Avoid big mistakes and ongoing error, which is costly in this business. Lack of information and guidance held me back in the beginning. Despite these hindrances, I earned $50,000 profit in my first year alone. Read on; you can make significantly more than that.

CHAPTER 3

PROVEN STRATEGY:
THE GOLDEN RULE & MORE

Gold buyers harbor many secrets, but one thing is apparent. They endure a bad reputation, like airline food or DMV customer service. They are well renowned for being poorly esteemed. They are pictured in a paradigm of dirty shops and desperate people. Just mentioning "gold buyer" may conjure cliché images. Some people imagine a slick-haired fast talker with eight gold rings and a patch of chest hair sticking out from his shirt.

The public's suspicion pervades. People assume that gold buyers take advantage of their sellers. This is a gross generalization but not baseless. The labels are true enough or, rather, true in enough cases that they continue to stick.

This negative connotation dissuades many potential patrons. In general, customers demand standards of appearance and conduct. This applies to most businesses. They want a quality product or service and a good experience. The *gold buyer* who provides this is worth his weight in precious metals.

Some sellers are actively searching for a buyer. Some already know or utilize a buyer but would switch to a better buyer. Some have been deterred from selling, or even searching, altogether. The last group will hold their metals indefinitely until an acceptable option arises.

This setting is like fertile ground for the careful gold buyer. Certain professional priorities will feed your business like Miracle-Gro. You don't need a green thumb to reap heaps of green, though.

Metal Man's slogan was, "(removed city)'s *BETTER* Gold & Silver Buyer!" That small phrase communicated a big message, and I worked to prove it true. Follow my strategy.

Firstly, a good name is your most valuable asset. It stands above other buyers like an NBA center among schoolchildren. Customers understand their disadvantage.

People need professionals to do things they can't or won't do themselves. Most sellers don't know what their metal is worth. They don't know how to use all your tools or formulas either. So they have to rely on a buyer if they want to sell. Therefore, they want a trustworthy professional—not a hack or a smooth operator. Consider how much you value the name of a good mechanic, real estate agent, or doctor.

As a novice I speculated that each customer would meet with me one time only. Why would they contact me again after selling? Why indeed? It is amazing how previous customers keep mining more metal. You might think it breeds in their jewelry boxes and dresser drawers.

The wheels start turning once you exceed their expectations with a rewarding transaction. Selling to a good gold buyer is easy. Easy money attracts people like red feeders attract hummingbirds. Furthermore, those who need cash delight to find a ready source of it. Suddenly, happy clients are sifting through their remaining items mentally sorting pieces into "keep" and "sell" categories.

A high percentage of them call for a second round of selling. Others invited me back as intermediaries—selling their friends' metals to me. Repeat business accounted for *at least* 25% of my income.

Couple that effect with the novelty value of knowing "the guy". Apparently, casual conversations frequently touch on the topic of selling gold. Somebody somewhere is probably even talking about it right now. Odds are that your satisfied customers will be privy to such conversations at some point. Everybody likes to feel "connected" or "in the know". Furthermore, friends want to help friends. Therefore, they will jump at the chance to exclaim, "I know just the guy for you to call!"

Word spreads quickly of outstanding businesspeople. Personal recommendations also carry more weight than marketing messages alone. Referrals are the gold buyer's boon.

This is how careless gold buyers shoot themselves in the feet. Not every transaction secures an endorsement. Some clients sell with mixed emotions to unprofessional buyers. They may yield to buyer pressure or want to avoid further hassle. Yet disgruntled clients are dead ends—burned bridges. They will not recommend, and often will warn others against, such buyers.

Most importantly, remember that your customers are *people*—not *targets*. Remember also that happy customers will prosper your business. Consequently, no transaction is totally successful without a satisfied seller.

A few sellers can't recognize a good buyer. They will feel cheated when they depart the transaction. This may be due to lingering distrust or unrealistic expectations. You *can't* change all of their minds. You *can* treat all of your customers well. The successful gold buyer crafts his image like a sculptor crafts his masterpiece.

Secondly, many buyers work in fixed locations. They stay in their buildings or booths. Conversely, you can mobilize.

A mobile gold buyer's customers can relax at home with a sense of security. More than a few sellers sat me at a table with their items and then returned to their televisions, kids, or household tasks. I simply alerted them later when I finished my work.

What about sell-by-mail companies? Calling the mobile buyer is even easier than ordering a jewelry mailer, completing the paperwork, and mailing it in. It is faster too. Convenience is king these days. In-home service can give you a huge competitive advantage.

Thirdly, you can out-price jewelers and the other types of buyers. Many sellers view jewelers as the best buyer option available. Two observations catalyze this thinking. Jewelers project a more elite image than pawn shops. They also offer face to face interaction whereas sell-by-mail entities cannot. However, they pay expensive overhead for their operations.

Fancy stores in prime locations cost big money. Contrastingly, mobile buyers avoid these liabilities. Hence they can pay more while retaining a larger profit margin. Jewelers typically pay more than other types of buyers. So, if you can beat their prices, you can beat them all.

I am not advising that you pay customers unreasonably high rates. You need to earn a living. Plus, part of the attraction to gold buying is its generous profitability. Competitive prices and high earnings need not be mutually exclusive goals, though. Each transaction can benefit both you and your customer.

Many, or most, gold buyers aim for every dollar on every deal. They first pitch a low-ball offer to test the seller. Some sellers meekly settle at this price; some haggle for a little more. Only the most knowledgeable and aggressive sellers get the best prices. The buyer has a distinct advantage in expertise and experience.

Offering different prices for different customers is modus operandi in many areas of business. I enjoy haggling and practice it whenever possible as a shopper. Some folks don't share that enthusiasm, however. Moreover, the gold buying business is unique. The common customer's total lack of knowledge stands alone from other commerce situations.

It's not like selling a car, for instance. Sellers can't simply look in a price book to find the actual value of their items. *To me* the gold buyers' sport of haggling seems more like bullying than a competitive match. The idea bothered me, and I knew it bothered many of the people I hoped to buy from.

As a result, I decided to treat every client as my grandmother. No, I didn't shout at them in their "good ears". Instead, I dealt with them straightforwardly as I hoped somebody would deal with my dear old granny. In fact, sometimes I actually bought from dear old grannies, and considered it a bit sacred. This personal pledge is why I invented the "No Haggle Guarantee" for Metal Man clients.

Metal Man guaranteed the same fair rates to every customer. The timid old lady was given the same great deal as the big, imposing man. Most clients didn't want to haggle. This unique promise assured them it was unnecessary. I marketed it as one more distinguishing feature of Metal Man. This policy can set you apart too.

Combine trustworthiness, convenience, and the best price (Figure B). It was my formula for success. It cannot substitute for knowledge or effective marketing. Nonetheless, a winning strategy is a key to any accomplishment. Think of this as the bedrock foundation for building an enduring gold buying business.

METAL MAN'S WINNING STRATEGY

Trustworthiness + Convenience + Best Price = $UCCESS

Figure B

Trustworthiness is the most important factor in your business equation. Convenience and strong pricing are secondary but complementary. This three-fold strategy was my golden goose, and I endorse it as the ideal. Nonetheless, readers can implement all or only part of this strategy.

Honesty and *high prices* may produce acceptable results without offering house calls. In that case, you should at least consider offering some other convenience instead. On the other hand, an honest and *convenient* buyer might find it unnecessary to pay more than other buyers. Just paying average prices could be adequate then, especially if you offer a fair price guarantee.

CHAPTER 4

UNDERGROUND NETWORK: REFINERIES

Commodities like precious metals and oil are listed on the Commodities Exchange, or "COMEX" for short. Think of it as the stock exchange for commodities. Pertaining to the gold buyer, it reflects market values for one troy ounce of each precious metal. For example, the displayed COMEX gold price is the current market value of one troy ounce (1 ozt) of pure (24K) gold. This price is referred to as "spot" or the "spot price".[$]

The COMEX is a publicly traded market. Therefore, metal prices fluctuate like stock prices. Consequently, you will both pay and receive different prices for metals at different times.

Mr. Gold Buyer is the middleman between John Q. Public and Acme Refinery. First, you buy customers' metals for a portion of spot value, or "rate". Then you sell them to a refinery at a higher rate. The difference between those

---

[$] Visit *www.usagold.com* for current spot prices.

amounts is your profit. If my business strategy is a golden goose, then a good refinery will be your cash cow.

Refineries are a secret to most people. The majority of customers aren't even familiar with the term "refinery". I never mentioned refineries when customers asked me what I did with the purchased metal. Most of the time I responded that it was proprietary information. Once in a while I said the items would get melted—but nothing else. Some assumed I was going to melt it myself; I saw no reason to correct the assumption.

Assays

An assay refers to the process of refining metal and paying for the amount of pure yield. Correctly or not, the term "assay" is used as both a noun and verb. You will send in a quantity for assay, and the refinery will assay it.

You will require a separate assay for each base metal but not for each variety. This means the refinery will assay silver and gold separately. However, 10K and 14K gold belong in the same assay.

Some refineries charge assay fees. Most pay according to a sliding scale. (See Table 4.1 for an example.) Others pay fixed rates but require minimum weights for assays. Refineries' policies vary; so also do gold buyers' preferences.

KARAT GOLD
PURCHASING SCHEDULE

Quantity	Rate
0–99 dwt	90%
100–199 dwt	95%
200–299 dwt	96%
300–499 dwt	97%
500 or more dwt	98%

Table 4.1

Lock-ins

Good refineries pay top dollar for your metal. The best refineries offer gold buyers a lock-in privilege. Your call initiates the action. When ready to sell you can "lock in", or affix to, the current spot price. This means they will pay you later according to what the spot price was when you called. Refineries that don't offer this service will lock in spot when they physically receive your assay.

Let's say you have 300 dwt of gold, and Acme Refinery pays a 95% rate. You call and lock in a 300 dwt gold assay when spot is $900. After refining your gold they will pay you 95% of $900, multiplied by the weight of pure yield. Now let's say your 300 dwt (15 ozt) assay yields 8.4 ozt of pure gold. Acme refinery will pay you $7182 minus fees, as demonstrated by Figure C.

ACME REFINERY SETTLEMENT

$900 (spot) x 95% (rate) x 8.4 ozt (yield) = $7182 (- fees)

Figure C

The lock-in option is a safety feature for you. You derived your buying price from the spot price when you bought. Without a lock-in you will lose money if spot falls significantly before your gold reaches the refinery. This is especially detrimental if you price competitively. A 25% profit margin offers a smaller buffer than a 50% margin.

Prices *could* rise in the interim instead. In that case, without a lock-in, your load would be worth more at assay time. It happens, but I am not a gambler. I prefer to know *that* my hard work will pay off and approximately *how much* it will pay.

A lock-in remains valid for several days. This works to the successful gold buyer's advantage. Whenever spot price began to drop, I locked in any amount in my possession preemptively. That prevented a monetary loss on what I had already purchased. If I wasn't ready to assay, I continued buying at the decreased prices for a few more appointments or a couple of days. Then I locked in the additional amount and delivered the whole batch to the refinery.

This brings up another point. You *can* request two lock-ins on one entire assay *but* only one lock-in per amount. In other words, you can lock in 100 dwt at $920 and another 100 dwt at $940 later. Then you would send in the whole 200 dwt load at once. However, you cannot lock in

100 dwt at $920, and then redo it at $940 if the price goes up. The refinery will calculate the yield value in proportion to each lock-in. In this former case they would pay 50% of the yield at $920 and the other 50% at $940.

Send in your assay as soon as possible after locking in; don't delay unnecessarily. Refineries sell your assay to their customers in advance. Therefore, they cannot afford to tolerate undependable gold buyers.

Your lock-in is a verbal contract to sell a specific amount at a specific price. Neglecting to submit it or submitting it late constitutes a broken contract. This also applies if your assay is significantly lighter than you stated. Your refinery may either rescind your lock-in privilege or refuse your future patronage over a broken contract.

Choosing the Right Refinery

My first refinery did not allow lock-ins. They also paid lower rates than other refineries but didn't charge fees. Most importantly, they didn't enforce a minimum weight even though my assay weights were minimal.

Choose the refinery that suits your present circumstances. Changes in your situation may lead you to a different refinery later. Nothing limits you to a single refinery either. Table 4.2 illustrates how multiple refineries may each serve a particular purpose best. At the very least, choose a back-up refinery. It provides a "Plan B" when your main refinery presents problems, like extended wait times.

EXAMPLE OF FACTORS IN CHOOSING A REFINERY

	Advantage	Disadvantage	Best for...
A	98% for gold assay 400+ dwt 95% for silver assay 80% outright for sterling Located nearby	$60 assay fee	Gold assay 400+ dwt Selling sterling outright for fast cash Silver assay if extra 6% over B negates the $60 fee
B	No minimums No assay fee 89% for silver assay	94% for gold	Gold assay <200 dwt Silver assay if $60 fee at A negates their 6% higher rate
C	95% for gold assay 200–399 dwt	$65 assay fee 96% for gold assay 400dwt+ 80% for silver assay	Gold assay 200–400 dwt if extra 1% over B negates the $65 fee

Table 4.2

Delivery to the Refinery

As you accumulate metals, store them safely in appropriate containers. Add each day's booty to the cache. Combine your scrap gold items together for one assay and your scrap silver together for another. Keep bullion and coins separate from non-like items. Group them together according to metal type and purity.

Fast forward to assay time. You want to sell, now. Maybe dwindling cash forces the issue, or prices threaten to fall. Perhaps you just deem the hoard big enough.

First, weigh your stockpile. Then call the refinery to lock in your assay/s. They will request your name and the metal type and weight for each assay. They also will dictate a confirmation number as a record; write it down. Choose your delivery method next.

Do you live within several hours of a refinery? You should consider personally delivering your metal. A short drive costs less than postage plus insurance. Even long drives cost less for heavy or valuable loads. Personal delivery also provides piece of mind: that value is immeasurable. Additionally, some refineries pay partial advances when you drop off your assay. Who knows? You might need some of that money for a big buy tomorrow.

Distant and busy buyers default to snail mail. Choose USPS (or your federal service), UPS, or FedEx (especially for international mail). Proper packaging is essential:

- ✓ Store metals in zipper bags or disposable plastic kitchen containers.

- ✓ Stack junk silver in paper coin wrappers, or use a strong bag for each denomination.

- ✓ Place individual numismatics in clear coin sleeves.

Crowd everything together in a box. Stuff the empty spaces with newspaper (or foam peanuts). Lastly, enclose an index card or computer printout with the essential details:

- ✓ Name
- ✓ Address
- ✓ Phone number
- ✓ Contents' description
- ✓ Confirmation number

Ensure that pieces don't poke through the exterior, shift around, or jingle. Whatever carrier you select, always purchase insurance. Again, *always* purchase insurance!

Skimping on insurance is a risky way to cut costs. Packages disappear every day. Protect your investment and sleep peacefully with insurance. Retain your insurance receipt until you receive your assay check.

Where to Find Refineries

Appendix C lists the best refineries I could find. It includes every company I used, along with others. All of them are actual refineries and not just large scale gold buyers. None of them compensate me in any way for their inclusion in this list.

You are not limited only to refineries in your home country. Several of these refineries invite international business. Granted—international shipping is more expensive and takes more time than the domestic option. Nevertheless, the payoff may outweigh the cost.

Visit their websites; read about them. Check their rates and pay scales. Call each of them to discuss their policies on lock-ins, minimums, and assay fees. You also need to know the shipping requirements for each refinery. Ask for any other pertinent information they can offer.

Keep in mind that prices may be negotiable. Some refineries set their prices in stone; others will negotiate if your assays are especially large or frequent. Even 1% extra is worth your effort. Unless you are some sort of gold buying prodigy, however, your initial assays will not impress. Set this as a long-term goal.

CHAPTER 5

PROVISIONS & PARAPHERNALIA, PART I: STANDARD EQUIPMENT

The successful gold buyer is half strategist, half scientist, and half tradesman. Carpenters need hammers, and plumbers need wrenches. Likewise, gold buyers require mission-specific tools. Just forego the bulky toolbox, and carry a briefcase or kitbag instead.

Metal Man's briefcase looked like a 007 prop. Furthermore, it was fully equipped. The self-contained mobile office featured a "secret agentesque" aluminum construction. In it, I neatly stored all the tools mentioned below, alongside marketing materials. The intriguing design garnered curious attention. Customers' compliments confirmed its professional impression.

Read about the primary tools of your trade below. A brief description follows each item. Visit my stores, The Gold Buyer Supplier (in the US, UK, and Canada), for a complete inventory of gold buyer supplies at low prices.$ Pick up the common items at your local department store or office supply store.

Pocket Scale (500 grams)

Digital scales vary in design but share common features. Select a 500-gram capacity scale that displays in 0.1g increments or smaller. This describes a basic pocket scale. The sensitivity, or margin of error, should be 0.1g or less. It must weigh in grams, pennyweights and troy ounces. Fortunately, most decent scales meet these standards. Purchase a calibration weight to frequently ensure your scale's accuracy.

The choice between a square or round weighing surface is purely personal preference. Some scales feature a removable lid. The lid flips over and doubles as a shallow dish to contain items. This prevents pieces from sliding off the flat surface during weighing.

I used a DigiWeigh scale—a safe choice. This is one common brand of digital pocket scale. The classic flip-open design protected the LCD. The square surface was perfect for weighing a small box full of scrap. Without the box, pieces would unravel over the sides and slide off.

I recommend including a small box along with your tools (listed below). Even so, I advise you to purchase a scale with a removable lid/dish. The dish doesn't hold much, but

---

$ Visit my website, and click on the links for The Gold Buyer Supplier.

it is part of the scale. Thus you won't forget to bring it with you. Occasionally, I forgot my box and was then ill-equipped for my appointment. In those instances I regretted my lack of an attached dish.

There are two things about scales you must never forget. First, make sure your scale is set to the correct unit of measurement. You don't want to pay per pennyweight, only to realize your scale was measuring in grams. Then you would have paid one-third more than you should have. Second, tare your scale properly when using a dish or box to hold items. The "tare" button sets your scale to zero; tare with the empty container on the scale before weighing anything. Otherwise, you will pay the customer for the weight of your container in addition to his metal. I already made both of these mistakes for you.

Acid Test Kit

You will employ the test kit contents to test metals. Proper use of the acids and stone accurately identify clients' items.[$] Testing can determine which pieces are phony, which are real, and their purities.

A starter kit includes six small bottles of nitric acid and a square test stone. The assorted bottles are diluted to various strengths. One bottle each is labeled for use on 10K, 14K, 18K, and 22K gold as well as platinum and silver. Some acids can be used on multiple metals or purities.

[$] Chapter 8 explains testing procedures.

The kits that don't include 22K gold and platinum acids are refill kits. Since platinum and gold above 18K are still less common, you will run out of the other four acids first. Then you can purchase a refill kit to avoid paying for unwanted acids.

Rubber Gloves

Though sold separately, rubber gloves serve as part of your test kit. You want to avoid skin contact with the nitric acid because it *eats* skin. The relatively weak 10K acid will produce yellow stains on fingers by the next day. The stronger acids sting within minutes and brown or blacken the spot within hours. One to two weeks later the discolored skin will peel off like a scab. Even a drop will produce these effects.

Your customers will watch the testing process, intrigued; your hands will be a focal point. So prevent stained and peeling hands. The colored stains make hands appear unwashed to observers, and peeling skin is simply gross. Errant drops are inevitable but plastics are impervious to acid. Therefore, thin rubber gloves are your best defense. Buy a box of them.

Horseshoe Magnet

A horseshoe magnet is an alnico magnet. The name "alnico" is derived from its alloy composition of aluminum, nickel, and cobalt. Alnico magnets are acclaimed for their superior strength over other magnets. You need a small horseshoe magnet for preliminary sorting purposes.

Precious metals are *non-magnetic*. Many of the metals present in costume and imposter jewelry *are magnetic*. Check items with a magnet before searching for stamps or testing.[$] This first step shortens the sorting process.

Slowly float the magnet back and forth over the items. It will not attract gold-filled items since copper is non-magnetic too. It will not attract vermeil either. Yet the magnet will attract most plated and costume jewelry pieces.[$] Afterward, you can proceed to examine and test the items.

Leatherman Tool

The Leatherman tool is like a Swiss Army knife on steroids. The pliers can bend open the prongs of jewelry settings to remove the gems they grasp. When a setting won't surrender, the tool can squeeze and twist the jewelry to free the stone. The file is stronger than a standard testing file: it cuts deeper faster and won't wear away. I even used the knife tips to untangle thin necklaces while staring through a loupe (mentioned next). A Leatherman is the perfect all-purpose tool for the successful gold buyer.

[$] Chapter 7 explains stamps and markings.

[$] Certain necklace and bracelet clasps each contain a small steel spring which holds the clasp closed. This will attract the magnet but the length, or body, of the item will not.

Jeweler's Loupe

A loupe, or "jeweler's loupe", is a magnifying lens. Picture the monopoly guy; the most common loupe design looks like his monocle. Others types of loupes are worn *over,* rather than *on,* the eye. Keychain models feature a flip-out design that is *held to* the eye by hand.

Gold buyers use loupes to examine small markings and other details. Loupes also enable better viewing of the testing process. With one you can place the acid more precisely and observe the acid reaction more clearly. Your loupe should provide 10 to 20 times magnification.

Holding a keychain loupe slows work by occupying one hand. Eye loupes require a squinting eye to secure them, which strains after a while. My preferred loupe clipped onto my eyeglasses and left my hands free to work. However, it clumsily popped off sometimes. A sturdy headband magnifier, which technically isn't a loupe, sits on the head and slides up and down over both eyes. Its drawbacks are its size and that customers will think you look like a mad scientist. You decide which option seems most fitting to you.

Some loupes boast an LED light which can be helpful in less than ideal lighting. For example, it can highlight markings. Conversely, a bluish LED also distorts colors. This can impede your examination and waste your money. For instance, you must be able to notice if there is green in an acid reaction and recognize when copper is an item's base metal. Both tasks rely on accurate color identification.

Calculator

This item doesn't require a lengthy explanation. You need a calculator to run the numbers. Just don't use your kid's SpongeBob calculator or a 1980's calculator watch. The first could cause embarrassment; the second complicates computation.

Small Box

You now know that some digital scales come complete with a small dish. Sans dish, the box is your only means of preventing items from spilling over or rolling off of the weighing surface. A small box also holds more than an integrated dish. Purchase a scale with a dish, but carry a small box too.

A small cardboard ring box or something similar will complement your scale. The straight, rigid sides restrain uncooperative pieces. Omega necklaces, for example, must be rolled up to fit on a scale. However, they will not stay rolled without containment. Such a box also holds larger loads than many standard lids/dishes.

Zip Bags

You will need separate containers to hold your purchases. Plastic zipper bags meet the need cheaply. At each transaction add the newly acquired items to your bag/s. Keep separate bags for gold and silver.

Use an empty bag for each transaction. It's best that customers don't know how much or how little business you conducted prior to them. Stock your supplies with both small and large bags.

Large Box

Zipper bags prove inadequate for some large purchases; they are too shallow to hold silver sets. Furthermore, whereas a huge score of coins might *fit* into a zipper bag, the bag isn't strong enough to *hold* it. A large cardboard box or plastic storage container can fill these roles. Bring it with you if you know you'll need it. Otherwise, leave it in your vehicle and excuse yourself to retrieve it when necessary.

Mileage Log

A mileage log documents business-related travel. You need a log unless you use separate vehicles for personal and business purposes. MapQuest, Google Maps, or a GPS can help you locate sellers' addresses and plan routes. They also specify the distance between points and trip totals. I documented these numbers in the mileage log.

All you need is a basic, small notebook. From left to right, write the date, receipt number (or other reason for travel), and miles traveled. Complete one entry per line. When a page fills up, calculate the total mileage for that page. Annotate it in the top corner. That will simplify your annual mileage calculations at tax time.

Uncle Sam allows you to deduct a specific monetary amount per mile traveled. The specific allowance increases most years. Competent tax preparers stay current with the changes. So keep track of your miles traveled; that figure, small or large, equals a deduction for you.

Receipt Book

Cash registers document money received. The receipt book records money paid out. Binder-type receipt books work well for non-mobile buyers. Meanwhile, mobile buyers value portable options. A standard small pad of fifty two-piece receipts sufficed for me.

I created a receipt for every transaction. This requires the customer's photo identification. First, detail the top portion with a full name, address, and driver's license or ID number. Next scribble a general item description, and fill in the payment amount. Lastly, ask the customer to sign the bottom of the receipt. The pink copy goes to the client; retain the white copy intact for your records.

The order of those final steps is essential. Customers signed *after* I took possession of the metal and *before* I paid. That way, sellers couldn't refuse to hand over my metal after receiving payment. They also couldn't accuse me of theft. I can't *know* if I avoided either of those scenarios. Still, that's better than *wishing* I had prevented a problem.

Ledger

Here again, we consider Uncle Sam. He requires every business to keep a complete set of records. No, your old Monkees albums don't qualify. Your business records will consist of a mileage log, receipts, and a ledger.$

Tax preparers use these records to calculate income. Their job includes finding all possible deductions for you, which minimize your tax liability. Good records make their job easier. Consequently, the end result will be as good as it can be for you.

The mileage log provides a total to calculate your mileage deduction. The *mileage log* entries are referenced by the ledger. The *receipts* evidence expenses but mainly prove the ledger. You need those items, but the *ledger* ranks highest. It provides a bird's-eye view of your business.

A ledger tracks expense and profit; by looking at it you know what you paid and made. The ledger will show if and how much your recent advertisement has impacted income. Even casual examination may help you recognize trends and seasons in your business. All of this knowledge can help you improve your operation's efficiency and success.

Develop a routine for maintaining your ledger. I updated my ledger after each appointment when time permitted. Otherwise, and most often, I updated it at the end of each workday. Record every business transaction in it—from buying gold to purchasing postage.

$ Your entire record of receipts includes your receipt book and store receipts from other business related purchases.

Label each page with the current month, and input each transaction in consecutive order. From left to right begin with the date. Next write a short description of the transaction. Instead of a description, you can simply fill in the receipt number to annotate a gold purchase.

There are two columns—one for income and one for expenses. Write the amount of the transaction in its proper column. A gold purchase belongs in the expense column. Meanwhile, a refinery check belongs in the income column.

Some months' records may exceed one page in length. Calculate the totals for each column on each page. As with your mileage log, list the totals at the top of their respective columns.

Figure your total income at the end of each month. Turn back to the leading page for that month. Then write the total somewhere conspicuous for easy reference. This makes it easy for your tax preparer to add the totals later—saving time (read paid hours). Begin the next month on the next new page.

Secrets of a Successful Gold Buyer

Every gold buyer should keep a copy of this book close by. Think of it as your gold buying manual. Imagine Metal Man riding shotgun, answering your questions and offering advice. It's like that, except you won't have to buy me lunch.

Tuck it into your glove compartment or briefcase. Refer to it when you forget something or want to review. Just don't let your clients see it!

List of Necessary Tools

Tool	Estimated Value
Digital Scale – 500g	$15–$30
Calibration Weight	$5
Acid Test Kit	$20
Rubber Gloves	$5
Horseshoe Magnet	$15
Leatherman	$50–$100
Jeweler's Loupe	$3–$10
Calculator	$10
Small Box	$1 (free with ring)
Zip Bags	$2
Large Box	$5
Mileage Log	$1
Receipt Book	$5
Ledger	$8
Secrets of a Successful Gold Buyer	Priceless!

Table 5.1

CHAPTER 6

Provisions & Paraphernalia, Part II: Advanced Equipment

This chapter introduces you to optional tools. They are optional in the sense that you can begin buying gold without them. Undoubtedly, growing gold buyers will obtain a few of them eventually.

This list is a primer—not exhaustive. I don't know your long-term business goals. *You* may not even know yet. Successful gold buyers can diversify in many directions. Different activities dictate different tool requirements. So the list below explains general considerations without lingering in any specific area of specialization.

As new buyers progress, they buy more frequently and bigger amounts. Certain devices facilitate larger operations. Busy buyers also acquire many desirable items (besides just scrap) at scrap prices. Reselling them outside of the refinery circuit involves additional equipment. Some buyers even branch out to deal with diamonds and gemstones. Once again, this endeavor necessitates more tools.

Postal Scale (10+ lb or 5+ kg)

A digital postal scale is preferable to a pocket scale sometimes. Big jewelry loads do not fit entirely on small scales. So, on a pocket scale, you can only weigh them in portions. Furthermore, some odd-shaped pieces do not fit on small scales at all.

A pocket scale can weigh most silverware, albeit awkwardly. To do that you weigh pieces individually and tally the totals. Pitchers and platters are too heavy for small scales. That forces you to estimate their weight. These methods are precarious and time-consuming. However, a postal scale can weigh everything at once.

Why not, then, simply replace the pocket scale with a postal scale? That won't work. Larger scales are made to measure heavier weights. Due to their greater maximum capacity, they are less precise than small scales. A 35 lb postal scale offers 6g sensitivity (approximately). That is an insignificant part of a silver set weighing 55 ozt. On the other hand it could erase your profit from a 20g necklace. Both scales perform similar but separate duties.

Postal scales don't offer troy measurements. Most American scales use the American system (British Units). Most other scales use the metric system. Both require you to convert the measurement to troy. However, scales with metric measurements save conversion steps

Americans, choose a US scale that can display in ounces—not just pounds and ounces. For example, it reads "49 oz" instead of "3 lb, 1 oz". Starting with an ounce measurement is like bypassing traffic. It saves time over converting pounds to ounces *before* converting to troy ounces. One less math step amounts to one less chance for error in your calculations too. To simplify the whole process, just buy a scale that displays in grams.

Digital Coin Sorter

The best time to purchase a coin sorter is ahead of time. Trust me. Counting and stacking several thousand dollars worth of silver coins is tedious. A digital coin sorter prevents that problem.[$] Nevertheless, they are imperfect. So you should recount every lot a few times and assume the lowest count.

When a customer hands you a sack of coins, drop it into the sorter. A digital sorter will sort and count your coins in short order. The machine will display the monetary total when complete.

Clients who bring you large amounts of coins are either collectors or investors. (Otherwise, they are the children or widows of said persons.) These silver coin enthusiasts are interested in silver coins only. For this reason, you will not find non-silver coins in most large junk silver loads.

You should spot check the coins, though. Examine some of them randomly—looking at dates to confirm silver

[$] Digital coin sorters don't accommodate old silver half dollars and dollar coins.

content. No check is necessary when dealing with sealed sacks or tubes.

Machines which sort and/or count 312 coins per minute cost around $100 online. They even shoot the coins into a small bucket or paper rolls. Life doesn't get any easier than this. Think about it: the machine can count and sort 312 mixed coins faster than *you* can roll 50 pennies. The profit on your first big purchase of junk silver will dwarf the equipment cost.

Electronic Gold Tester

Some buyers use electronic gold testers. Users fasten the attached electrodes or alligator clips to the metal item in question. Testers "work" by measuring electrical conductivity.

I researched these testers before starting Metal Man. I found mixed reports. Many users assert that the testers don't work or are undependable. It seems that nothing can replace the tried and true visual exam and acid test. I like neither wasting money nor complicating easy things. So I never worked with an electronic tester. Newer models may hold potential, though. Current testers include Golden Touch, Mizar, and Tri-Electronics models.

Prong Lifter

A professional acquaintance once insisted that I purchase a prong lifter. This is a small, flat, rectangular tool.

It is close in size to a stick of gum. Several filigrees are cut into each end; it looks like a factory second can opener. The tool is made to pry open the prongs on gemstone settings.

I never mastered the frustrating prong lifter. My Leatherman suited me better than this tool. The Leatherman was harder on jewelry but easier on my nerves.

No matter what you use, remove nice gems from jewelry you intend to assay. Many pieces contain quality gemstones. The stones are worth nothing to the refinery and about 10% more to a jeweler. However, you may find a use or market for them in the future. If nothing else, give them to somebody special; she will consider them treasure.

Ultrasonic Cleaner

Ultrasonic cleaners clean jewelry and some gemstones. They range from pint-size personals to 3-liter (litre) commercial units. The body consists of a tub, lid, and timer.

Place the soiled items into the tub. Next pour in a 50/50 water and vinegar solution, fully immersing the items.[$] Plain water is less effective; vinegar acts as a solvent. Plug in the unit, set the timer, and wait. When finished, air dry the gems and wipe the other items with a jewelry cloth.

These machines emit ultrasonic frequencies which remove dirt through agitation. Picture the Sonic Brush toothbrush if you have seen commercials about it. Ultrasonic cleaners can put a shine on any jewelry pieces you intend to

[$] Commercial solutions and other home recipes are also available.

resell. They also restore the brilliance of quality gems. Beware; some gems may not withstand ultrasonic cleaning.[$]

Gem Scale (100g)

This small-scale scale is ideal for weighing loose gemstones—which you remove from jewelry. A gem scale is precise. Commonly, these offer a maximum capacity of only 100g and boast 0.01g sensitivity. Most importantly, it can display weight in carats. You can resell your loose gemstones to the public, unload them on jewelers in bulk, or garnish jewelry displays with them.

Gem Gauge (Diamond Gauge)

Have you seen any advertisements for gemstone jewelry lately? Do you know what piece of information they most often include? I'll give you a hint: it's the gem weight. Okay, that wasn't a hint, was it?

Specifying the gem weight is standard procedure. This applies to full-page magazine ads as well as tiny classified ads. Jewelry buyers want to know gem weight like car buyers want to know vehicle horsepower, or fuel economy (depending on who is buying). So you need to ascertain gem weights in pieces you plan to resell.

[$] This book focuses on gold buying—not gemstones. For specifics, visit my website and proceed to the *Gemstone Guide*.

A gem scale weighs *loose* gems. Conversely, a diamond gauge, or "gem gauge", determines the size of a jewel *in its setting*. Numerous designs are available, but they all share the important component—the cutouts.

The cutouts range in shape and size. Each is labeled with a carat measurement. Slide a gemstone along the gauge. Decide which cutout fits over that stone without extra space or overlap. The number beside the cutout tells you the approximate size. Gem cuts vary in depth, though, so same gems with the same size face may differ in weight.

Extensive involvement with diamonds and gemstones requires a host of other tools. Incidentally, this also applies to watch dealing and watch/jewelry repair. All three offer expansion opportunities for the successful gold buyer. Research these topics if they interest you.

Graduated Ring Mandrel (Ring Stick)

A ring mandrel demonstrates a ring's size. The 10 inch (25 cm) conical metal or plastic stick widens toward the handle. (Or you could say it tapers toward the end.) The mandrel is marked with graduated measurements—ring sizes. Insert the mandrel through the ring. Slide, do not force, the ring down until it fits snugly. The line where the ring stops represents its size. Use a ring stick to determine the sizes of your resale rings.

Finger Gauge (Ring Sizer)

A ring stick measures the ring, but a finger gauge measures the finger. A finger gauge set is no more than a collection of labeled metal or plastic rings. The rings vary in ½ or ¼ sizes. Slip a finger through one gauge at a time like the mandrel through a ring. Choose the best fitting gauge. Its label shows that finger's size. A ring sizer helps you determine which of your resale rings fit an interested customer.

Red Book

The "Red Book", by R.S. Yeoman, is the gold standard in coin price guides. Its formal title is, *A Guide Book of United States Coins: The Official Red Book*. Each year brings a newly updated edition. It offers a wealth of coin information including price lists, photos, and tips. Buyers in other countries can acquire, as an alternative, *Standard Catalog of World Coins,* by George S. Cuhaj.

Frequently, clients' jewelry comes mixed with miscellaneous coins. Some of those coins are surprisingly valuable. Conversely, some very old coins look rare but are worth little. You need to know which is which and what price to offer. The Red Book lists each coin's retail value.

The Red Book displays several prices for each coin. The different prices correspond to different grades. A grade refers to the condition of a coin. A worn coin receives a low grade and is not worth as much as the same coin in pristine condition. The book itself offers guidance on coin grades.

Disregard book prices for common bullion coins. Gold and silver coin values are pinned to spot price. A 1 ozt Gold Eagle is worth approximately the same as 1 ozt of gold at any given time. Most of them do not hold numismatic value, though they sell at a premium.

The publisher can't print a price guide with a blank bullion section. So they calculate values according to spot price around the date of publish. By now you know that spot fluctuates; bullion prices do not stay static. Therefore, bullion values will rise or fall by the time you read the book. They will also change every time you check it.

Follow the book prices when reselling coins to the public. However, you are considered a coin dealer when reselling to coin dealers. Then you can only expect dealer pricing; dealer prices run lower than retail prices.

You can consult a grey sheet for dealer prices.[$] It's probably only worth the extra trouble if you buy a lot of coins, though. I didn't hassle with the grey sheet. Instead, I just dialed my trusted coin dealer. I asked his price on every coin before I offered to buy it from the customer.

[$] Visit *www.greysheet.com* for more information.

Optional Tools List

Tool	Estimated Value
Postal Scale – 35lb	$30
Digital Coin Sorter (non-commercial)	$100
Electronic Gold Tester	$100–$500
Prong Lifter	$10
Ultrasonic Cleaner (small)	$30
Gem Scale	$30–$50
Gem Gauge	$10
Graduated Ring Mandrel (plastic)	$5
Finger Gauge Set (plastic)	$5
Red Book	$17

Table 6.1

CHAPTER 7

PRELIMINARY INVESTIGATIONS: MARKINGS

Rarely does a *fine* gold or silver item lack a stamp of some sort. Often, even costume jewelry bears identification. The secret is what markings mean and where to look for them.

The successful gold buyer is multilingual. Besides understanding professional terminology he is proficient in the language of markings. He can interpret the various numbers, letters, and combinations thereof. Study the following tables to learn common markings and their meanings.

Where can you find markings? The locations vary according to each category of items. The descriptions (following the tables) provide specific details.

Gold Markings & Explanations

Marking	Meaning	Remarks
K	Karat	Preceded by number indicating purity (ex. "14K")
KP	Karat Plumb	Term used to mean "exact", preceded by number
417	10 Karat	
585	14 Karat	
K.P., GP, GEP, HGP, HGE, EP, GE	Gold Plated	Variations meaning standard and heavy gold plate and electroplate[$]
KGF, GF, 1/20	Gold Filled	1/20 represents the gold content by weight, may show "12K 1/20 GF"
925	Gold Plated Sterling	Called "vermeil"

Table 7.1

$ "EP" can be found on gold plated and silver plated items. The two varieties are easily discerned though. Typically, only yellow gold is used for plating. Furthermore, white gold plated items may also bear additional markings.

Silver Markings & Explanations

Marking	Meaning	Remarks
925, STER, Sterling, Mexico	Sterling	May show "Mexico" along with one of the other markings
900, Coin Silver, Pure Coin	Coin Silver	Found on silverware, indicates 90% content (as used in coins) rather than 92.5% sterling
800	800	Found on silverware or European jewelry
EP, EPS, EPNS	Silver Plated	Variations meaning electroplate and electroplated nickel silver
ONEIDA, Rogers, Triple Silver, International Silver, Community Silver	Silver Plated	Found on silverware, Indicate manufacturer

Table 7.2

Other Markings & Explanations

Marking	Meaning	Remarks
CHINA	Not real anything	May be stamped into the item or an affixed transparent sticker
MONET	Costume jewelry	Usually stamped on an oval charm attached to clasp, suspect all other unmarked items in the load to be costume jewelry too

Table 7.3

Necklaces

The clasp is the most commonly stamped part of a necklace. The clasp may be stamped on its side and even on its small spring-loaded tooth. A small ring holds the clasp to one end of the necklace. Additionally, the clasp clips onto a similar ring at the other end of the necklace. One or both of these rings may display stamps too. Fine pendants should be stamped separately, somewhere on their backs.

Bracelets

Chain and link bracelets mimic necklaces. Look for markings on the clasp, tooth, and connector rings. Additionally, each separately acquired charm on a charm bracelet should be stamped. Markings on bangle and cuff bracelets can be found somewhere on the inside surface or rim.

Watches

I can't count how many customers elicited my smile with their gold watches. The smile was not of joyful discovery, though. Instead, it politely held back a laugh. No offense intended; it's just funny.

More often than not their "gold" watches sported logos like Guess and Casio. A real gold watch costs much more than $150. Real gold doesn't fade away or chip off to reveal a silver color underneath. They probably knew these things, but the prospect of the big payoff clouded their reasoning faculties.

Clients want the gold buyer to look at everything that *might be* gold. So they throw watches into the pile despite the "Stainless Steel" stamps. Meanwhile, they cross their fingers and wait for your pronouncement. Most gold watches that clients offer you are *gold color* only.

Real gold watches are worth a bundle. True: not all expensive watches are gold. Also true: some watchmakers produce both fine and fashion watches. In my experience, however, people who buy gold watches *know* their watches are gold. So don't get your hopes up if a customer isn't sure.

First, determine the maker. The examination stops at "Casio" or "Guess", for instance. Search for markings on the case backing, clasp, and inside surface of the band. Assume replaceable bands are non-gold until proven otherwise.

You may decide to resell some fine watches. So test carefully, if you need to, in an inconspicuous area on the watch. Damage will nullify a fine watches resale value.

Disassembling a fine watch is dangerous. One wrong move can send pieces flying like Jiffy Pop. (Most mistakes would be less visually amusing but equally regrettable.) Still, you can't just weigh a watch and pay according to its total weight. You need to subtract the weight of the non-gold parts from the total weight. On the other hand, you don't want to dismantle the watch if you can resell it. Save the mechanisms from the watches you scrap. They can be useful when you encounter this situation.

Imagine you have a client's valuable gold watch in front of you. Look through your saved mechanisms for one which resembles that in the gold watch. Then weigh it. Its weight serves as a solid estimate for the gold watch's mechanism. Subtract that weight from the weight of the gold watch. Further deduct 1.5g or 1 dwt for the crystal.[$] The remaining total represents the approximate gold weight in the gold watch.

Rings

Class rings (generally 10K) were the most common type of ring I bought. They seem like a must-have at graduation but lose significance after a decade. Wedding bands (usually 14K) ran a close second—a harsh reality of gold buying. I bought enough of both that, eventually, I could guess their values by sight alone. Rarest was the gaudy cocktail ring brandishing one large gem or a colorful bouquet. They symbolize a bygone era now but are bounteous sources of loose gems.

Most rings display their markings prominently on the inside rim. Therefore, smooth bands offer the easiest task. However, a ring with an elevated face can present complications. For example, a gemstone ring may contain a hollow cavity behind the gem mount. Sometimes you can find the stamp there, even if the rough surface camouflages

[$] The crystal is the glass shield that covers the watch face.

the impression. This applies to other rings with a concave design (behind the face or main feature) as well.

If you *know* a ring is gold but can't find the stamp to prove it, ask how old it is. Often the client will say it was a parent's ring, worn for a lifetime. Years of wear can rub away any markings on a ring's inside rim. It's like how a stream rounds out a square rock. The difference is that markings rub away in (maybe) 40, instead of 400, years. This phenomenon also explains some partial or indistinguishable markings.

Earrings

More than any other jewelry items, the markings on earrings can be downright miniscule. Earrings are usually marked on the back surface or on the post. Hopefully your client cleans her earrings first. Otherwise, through your loupe, you will observe a blob of greasy build-up in grotesque detail. It may conceal a marking; wipe it away (Eeeww!) for a proper examination. Hoop earrings may be stamped on the inside perimeter if not on the post.

Hollow hoops are real gold—usually. Firstly, solid gold hoops would be too heavy; women want dangly *earrings* not dangly *earlobes*. Secondly, they would cost too much; hollow hoops look solid but contain less gold. This hollow construction can be found with other jewelry items also, but less often.

The earring backing is a separate item; treat it as such. Backings are frequently lost and replaced or else intermingled and inadvertently switched. There are two main kinds of backings. One is cylindrical or conical with a hole through the middle. There is no way to stamp this. The other is disc-like with two circles curled underneath it. Look for a stamp on its face. Lastly, the clip-on earrings in your pile are costume jewelry forty-nine times out of fifty.

Pins and Brooches

I want to avoid possible confusion of terms here. A "pin" is both a jewelry item and a part that secures said jewelry item to the clothing. In the explanation below, "pin" means jewelry piece. Meanwhile, the pin on the pin is a "nail". Okay? Read it again. Now let's proceed.

Unfunny but Relevant Joke

Q: Where is the marking on a pin or brooch?

A: Wherever you find it. (Badaboom!)

Figure D

My bland joke refers to the wide variation of design from one pin or broche to another. These items stick on a shirt and look like flowers, butterflies, or abstract art. There is no size requirement or *size limit!*

The nail is steel for strength, so that isn't marked. If the piece features a flat spot on the back, check it out.

Otherwise, grab your magnifying glass, Sherlock; the clue could be anywhere.

I never saw the same pin twice, but I can classify some of them as employee pins. Employee pins are small and flat with a nail sticking straight out of (perpendicular to) the back. The face either bears a company logo or some strange symbol that only your customer understands. Companies give them to employees to celebrate an anniversary, or as individual commendations.

It's a big pill to swallow when you tell a client that her "20 years with Acme Manufacturing" pin is only gold plated. Being a gold buyer means breaking the bad news sometimes. Most employee pins are 10K gold, gold plated, or simply non-gold. Few of them are 14K gold. The flat back surface bears the stamp.

Silver Sets

Silverware is one of the most common items that callers and clients ask about. Unfortunately, almost all of it is plated. The vast majority of fine silverware *is stamped* to indicate sterling or coin silver composition.

Even when marks have worn off of some pieces (knives, commonly), other pieces in the same set still bear marks. You will see many kinds of stamps. Nevertheless, the piece probably is not silver if you don't see some type of familiar silver stamp. Additionally, gold flatware is plated unless you are buying it from the Queen of England.

As with watches many customers insist on showing the gold buyer their "silverware". Unlike watches, even plated silverware is handed down in families through generations. So customers often don't know how much it cost or where it came from. They also mistakenly believe it is sterling because it is old or tarnished. This mistake is little trouble for you if you also buy their jewelry. However, making a special trip for, what turns out to be, a silver plated set wastes your time.

Whenever potential clients called about silverware, I taught them a quick lesson about markings. "It is silver if it is stamped 'silver', '925' or 'sterling'. It isn't silver if it has no stamp or is stamped 'Rogers', 'Oneida' or anything else."

I also listed more in-depth information on Metal Man's website FAQ page. I directed customers there for a full explanation if the abridged version didn't decide the issue. This strategy helped me avoid most wild goose chases—for silverware at least.

Sterling flatware exhibits markings on the handles. This includes place settings as well as the oversized serving pieces. Forks and spoons usually bear their stamps on their necks. Find their stamps on the back of the thinnest part of the handle, near the work end. Knife markings can be found on the handle's underside, near the blade.

Knife blades are made of stainless steel for strength. Parts of large serving pieces also are steel. So ignore the "stainless steel" inscriptions on these parts. The piece may still be silver.

The round silver handles of knives and some large serving pieces are *hollow*. The silver handle is a thin wrapper filled with plaster.[$] The plaster secures the steel blade in place and weights the handle. The round handle provides a better grip for cutting and serving than a flat handle. Meanwhile the filling spares unnecessary silver just as hollow gold hoops spare gold.

The silver wrapper is slightly thicker than heavy duty aluminum foil. It weighs little without the plaster, but don't expect to disassemble it at your appointment (as the client gawks incredulously). Estimate 7 or 8 grams for each piece with a round handle.

Refineries require the removal of plaster for assaying. It pollutes their process. For this task you will need two pairs of pliers and ten pounds of patience.

Grab the blade with one set of pliers and the handle with the other. Twist back and forth in opposite directions—alternating clockwise and counterclockwise. Also squeeze the handle methodically with the pliers. Squeeze, rotate, and repeat. You want to break up the plaster inside without flattening the handle. When the blade dislodges, some of the crumbled plaster will fall out. Continue with the pliers until you empty the handle of plaster. Some round handles contain lead or another metal instead of plaster. Then you can remove only the blades but not the filler metal.

[$] I discovered this fact too late—*after* excitedly buying my first silver set. The plaster content in the handles erased my profit.

Platters and Tea Sets

You can identify a steel or silver plated platter with your eyes closed. Hold it out in front of you. Non-silver platters feel like their loaded with bricks.

Non-silver platters are heavy and solid. Authentic sterling platters are thin and pliable—no thicker than they need to be. Silver platters and tea sets are marked on the underside—in the center or on the rim.

Dental Material

Yellow crowns (*metallic* yellow—not *plaque* yellow) are gold. Many buyers pay a standard 14K rate for these although some may be closer to 16K gold. Testing can be difficult; the other metals present may embellish the result. Some silvery bridges are composed of chromium cobalt and other hard metals which are impervious to your acid.

Everything Else

Successful gold buyers will see more items than those listed here. I have purchased other *marked* items like gold trinkets and silver picture frames.[$] I also have declined offers of gold bench scrap, melted silver lumps, and more.[$] Unusual items (like these last two) introduce higher risk to a gold buyer unless he pays a pittance.

[$] Silver candlesticks contain mostly plaster

[$] Bench scrap is a byproduct of jewelry making.

You'll develop a sense of where to look for markings. So check obvious places first. Practice caution with unmarked items. Above all, *do not buy anything you don't understand.*

CHAPTER 8

INTERROGATION TECHNIQUES: TESTING

Knowing how to properly test items is fundamental for a successful gold buyer. Performing the test is only half of the work; correctly interpreting the reaction comprises the other half. The results determine what you buy and what you leave behind.

Visual and digital examinations sometimes establish *probability,* but only acid testing *proves* purity. *Most* fine gold and silver items bear stamps. *Most* of those stamps are accurate. Nonetheless, successful gold buyers seek profit on *all* pieces they purchase. Testing weeds out worthless pieces and correctly identifies the rest.

The general process is called an "acid test". The two main kinds of acid tests include a scratch test and a destructive test. The third kind, a comparison test, is only used for 21–24K gold. Read the overviews to acquaint yourself with the two main tests. Then study the tables for step-by-step instructions for testing common alloys.

Testing will help you avoid wasting money *and* missing opportunities:

- Some jewelry repair parts are unmarked or not made of precious metal.

- Years of wear or use rub markings off rings and silverware.

- Prior to 1982 it was legal to stamp "14K" on 13.5K gold.

- Custom-made jewelry may be unmarked.

- American Indian silver jewelry may be unmarked.

- Dental gold and some other items are always unmarked.

- Some bogus items are marked and look deceptively real.

Do you know how bankers and others learn to detect counterfeit money? They study real money. In the same way, a gold buyer's experience with real gold and silver helps him recognize non-precious items. Bankers don't rely solely on their training, though. They often use black lights and special markers for extra protection. Likewise, a successful gold buyer liberally tests with acid. If unsure about an item, to any degree, it is best to test. For bankers *and* gold buyers, forgoing the test always involves some amount of risk.

This next nugget of advice may save you from a scam someday. Let's imagine you are sitting with a customer and just tested a valuable gold necklace. It looked real and passed the test. So you make an offer. The client says he isn't willing to sell for that price. Then he takes the item and puts it into his pocket. You inform him that your price is a good price; the necklace is nice but not worth more. He seems to change his mind and gives you the necklace back. Before you pay for that necklace, you better *test it again!*

Don't be duped by the bait-and-switch. Scammers will bait you with a real necklace and switch it with a nearly identical phony. Some honest customers will be ambivalent about selling. However, they usually don't remove items from your sight. They usually don't even remove their items from the table. So treat any item as new that has left your sight. In fact, treat it as a suspicious item to test.

This is not a lesson I learned personally—partly due to my choice of clientele. Nevertheless, I was warned by an acquaintance who narrowly avoided the error. So I am passing the warning on to you. Some less specialized buyers in my area were taken by this trick.

Primary Examination

Commence the examination process by spreading the client's items out in front of you. Float your magnet over them. Remove any piece that *completely* sticks to your magnet. Toss (okay, *place*) them in a "fail" pile.

The springs inside many clasps are steel. Replacement connector rings also may be plated or steel. Don't dismiss a piece just because the clasp or connector ring sticks.

Plated and filled items do not warrant separate purchase. Their gold content is negligible. Oftentimes customers offered them to me along with fine pieces. In those cases, I included them in my takeaway without paying extra. My rates were already high—no need to offer a quarter for a necklace worth fifty cents. Some pieces had sentimental value to clients, though. In those cases I advised the customer to keep the item. Why not advise your customers the same? Such items are barely worth extending your arm for and picking up. Plus, the kind gesture builds good will.

Look through your loupe for purity markings. Remove items that are obviously real. Organize them in like "pass" piles according to base metal and purity. Next, remove filled and obviously non-precious items. Condemn them to the "fail" pile along with the magnetic pieces you already quarantined. Lastly, the remaining marked and unmarked pieces head to the "test" pile.

Don your rubber gloves if you will use them. Proceed to test each item in the test pile. Follow the instructions below.

Avoid breathing the acid fumes: they are caustic. The largest amount of smoke results from fake pieces tested with strong acid. So don't lean directly over items while testing. Otherwise, any resulting smoke will rise straight into your nostrils. Sneezing, coughing, and animated, involuntary facial spasms may result. Additionally, you will have to excuse your tears to your concerned and bewildered client.

Continually separate the tested items as you go. Add each item to either the pass or fail pile. Upon completion you will move on to weighing and calculating value.

Tests

A scratch test causes little damage compared to a destructive test. Nonetheless, you should inform your client before performing either test. Explain why you need to test—to determine or confirm purity before paying. Then ask permission. Some sellers will hesitate to allow it. Kindly remind the customer it is a necessary step for every buyer. Emphasize that you will pay for the pieces that pass.

Scratch Test

Hold the metal item firmly in your hand. You want part of it, preferably an edge, to stick out between your thumb and index finger. Scratch, or scrape, it against the test stone surface. Scratch back and forth several times in a short straight line. It's the same motion as erasing pencil marks, but more forceful.

Your goal: transfer a streak of the metal onto the stone's surface. A hard scratch accomplishes this. A hard scratch also digs below the thin surface of plated and filled items. On the other hand, a soft scratch can yield a false positive when it does not reach the base metal underneath.

Next apply a drop of acid to the streak. You can determine the item's purity by the acid reaction. Expect any of four basic results. The acid will bubble green, or the streak will turn brown, disappear, or remain unchanged. If any streak disappears the item either contains no fine metal or is plated or filled.

Destructive Test

The destructive test digs deeper than the scratch test. Therefore, it detects plated and filled items better than scratching. It is the preferred way to test metal lumps and nuggets for the same reason. Additionally, large items like silver tea sets make scratch testing awkward. Then the destructive test offers the advantage of convenience. Lastly, it serves as a final ruling. It can prove, disprove, or clarify ambiguous scratch test results. The disadvantage is that it renders fine items non-resalable and other items unusable.

Hold the item firmly while sawing into it with a file. Cut a notch in the piece. (If your fingernail can hook into the notch, it's deep enough.) Then drip one drop of acid into the cut. As with the scratch test, the reaction will demonstrate the purity.

Fluorescent lights or poor lighting can obscure the color of the acid reaction. Work around this issue with a white tissue or napkin. Blot the acid site. Then look at the napkin to see if it the wet spot is transparent or contains green traces.

10K Scratch Test

Scratch the item against the stone. Then apply 10K acid to the streak.	
If nothing happens	≥10K
If the streak stays but fades to brown	Move to destructive test

Table 8.1

10K Destructive Test

File into the item. Then apply 14K acid to the cut.	
If nothing happens	≥14K
If the site turns brown but nothing else happens	10K
If the site turns brown and produces one or two green bubbles after 10 seconds	9K when marked
If the site turns brown and produces numerous green bubbles after 10 seconds	8K when marked
If the site turns brown and bubbles green profusely	≤7K (not gold if unmarked 7K)

Table 8.2

14K Scratch Test

Scratch the item against the stone. Then apply 14K acid to the streak.	
If nothing happens	≥14K
If the streak loses some brightness and eventually turns rusty yellow	13.5K
If the streak stays but fades to brown	10K

Table 8.3

14K Destructive Test

File into the item. Then apply 14K acid to the cut.	
If nothing happens	≥14K
If the cut loses some brightness and eventually turns rusty yellow	13.5K
If site turns brown but nothing else happens	10K

Table 8.4

18K Scratch Test

Scratch the item against the stone. Then apply 18K acid to the streak.	
If nothing happens	≥18K
If streak stays but fades to brown	≤14K

Table 8.5

18K Destructive Test

File into the item. Then apply 18K acid to the cut.	
If nothing happens	≥18K
If site turns brown but nothing else happens	≤14K

Table 8.6

21–24K Scratch Test

Scratch the item against the stone.	
24K gold can't bite into the stone. If the item does not leave a smooth, even streak	24K
If item leaves a normal streak, apply acid to the streak.	
If nothing happens	22K
If streak stays but eventually turns rusty yellow	21K
If streak stays but turns brown	≤18K

Table 8.7

Comparison Test (21–24K)

Scratch the item against the stone. Scratch a 22K or 24K gold coin alongside the first streak. Apply platinum acid to both streaks.	
If the streak from the coin fades first	Item is higher karat than coin
If streaks fade at same rate	Item is same karat as coin
If the streak from the item fades first	Item is lower karat than coin

Table 8.8

Gold Filled Scratch Test

Scratch the item against the stone. Scratch the same part of the item against the stone again, alongside the first streak. Scratch it again alongside the second streak. Then apply 14K acid to all three streaks.	
If the second and/or third streak fades or disappears	Gold plated or filled
If nothing happens	≥14K
If all streaks turn brown, but nothing else happens	10K

Table 8.9

Silver Scratch Test

Scratch item against the stone. Then apply 18K acid to the streak.	
If streak turns intensely silver-blue	Strong silver content, move to destructive test
If streak turns blotchy and uneven blue	Silver plated

Table 8.10

Silver Destructive Test #1

File into the item. Apply 14K acid to the cut.	
If site turns whitish or milky-gray color	≥90% (probably sterling)
If site turns darker gray	±80%
If green bubbles form	≤60%
If site bubbles green profusely	Silver plated or not silver

Table 8.11

Silver Destructive Test #2

File off a portion of the item's surface. (Exposed area must be wide enough to accommodate one drip of acid. Acid must not touch any part of the unfiled surface.) Then apply red silver acid to the exposed area.	
If the acid turns red	≥90% (purer silver turns brighter red)
If the acid turns brown	≤80%
If the acid turns green	≤50%

Table 8.12

A Note about Test Results

A successful gold buyer does not examine items hastily. However, he must complete his task within a reasonable time frame. Otherwise, he risks looking incompetent or wearying his clients. This forces a hard choice sometimes, in the interest of expedience.

You may find yourself unable to confidently identify an item. The quick test yields inconclusive results and you don't know why. You retest it and reach the same impasse. You must either buy it knowing it might be worthless (or just worth less) or reject it knowing it might be real. If you buy it, plan to retest it later at your leisure. Do not combine this bag with your main load now. Wait until after a satisfactory retest.

This is an opportunity to practice testing. Later, after work, you can take as much time as you need to retest. Reaching a conclusion about this item will sharpen your skills with similar items or results in the future. The following story illustrates another benefit.

One of my first customers was a businessman with numerous connections. First, he sold me his own high quality jewelry. Afterward, he began selling other clients' items to me as an intermediary. Not all of their pieces were comparable to his. I didn't realize that right away, though.

If test results were inconclusive (I was still learning), I usually gave his people the benefit of the doubt. I also used to combine my purchases in big bags after each deal. Eventually, I realized worthless pieces were infiltrating my purchases. Yet it was difficult at day's end to remember which obscure gold necklace belonged to whom.

I began segregating separate purchases. I retested items at home. Only afterward did I combine them all. Soon this revealed the source of my problem—the businessman.

It wasn't *his* fault; *I* was the professional. Nonetheless, it taught me to approach subsequent purchases through him more suspiciously. After that, I was more apt to reject a piece than to buy it with doubts. The practice of keeping bags separate saved me from wasting more money.

CHAPTER 9

DECRYPTION: CALCULATING VALUE

Calculating value is the most technical aspect of gold-buying. Consequently, the formulas may look intimidating at first glance. Don't worry. I never understood algebra in school. Despite my best efforts I just couldn't wrap my brain around it. I also thought it would never prove useful, but I was wrong. These equations are both simple and essential.

Read and re-read this chapter. You will use these equations every time you buy. The repetition will teach you in time, but you can lean on your notes in the beginning. A successful gold buyer commits these formulas to memory as soon as possible.

The Beginning

You must weigh items in order to calculate their value. Throughout the testing process you separated fine items into like piles. Next eject any large worthless "gems" (with your Leatherman tool) which remove easily. Then weigh each pile. Deduct an estimated weight of remaining gemstones and glass pieces. Use that final number to assess value by implementing the methods below.

Items like turquoise, onyx, amber, and glass are frequently large and always worthless. Leaving them intact will pad the item/load weight unnecessarily. Don't waste time struggling; just take out the easy stuff. Many jewelry loads will include pieces adorned with quality precious stones too. Leave them in for now. Decide what to do with them later, at your convenience.

Some sellers will ask if you can remove the gemstones for them. It's your call; you have a few options. First, you can grant the request. You ought to warn them that you cannot guarantee a successful removal. Second, charge a fee. Only those with adequate expertise should consider this option, because the buyer assumes liability. Third, you can tell them you don't remove gems. Respectfully inform them that the stones are eye candy but hold no resale value.

Common Measurements

Let's start with measurements. Gold buyers use several common units of measurement. Well, they are common to gold buyers. The troy measurements are rarely encountered by the general public. Table 9.1 provides explanations, abbreviations, and relevant conversion values for each unit.

Basic Units of Measurement

Unit	Abbr.	Explanation	Value
Carat	ct	Standard unit of weight for gemstones	0.2g
Gram	g	Standard unit of weight in metric system	0.64 dwt
Pennyweight	dwt	Standard unit of weight for precious metals, troy	1.55g
Ounce	oz.	Basic unit of weight in American system	28.35g
Troy Ounce	ozt	Larger weight unit for precious metals, related to dwt, quoted by COMEX	20 dwt, 31.1g
Pound	lb.	Largest common unit of weight in American system	16 oz.
Troy Pound	lbt	Largest common weight unit for precious metals	12 ozt

Table 9.1

Conversions

As mentioned in Chapter 7, some postal scales don't use troy measurements. Nevertheless, you will utilize a postal scale at some point. Additionally, some sellers will call you for a price quote after weighing their items on a post office's scale. In both cases you will need to translate the total weight in order to calculate a price.

The examples below demonstrate how to convert to troy measurements from other systems. From within the American system, convert *ounces* to pennyweight (for gold) or to troy ounces (for silver). Convert to ounces first, from pounds and ounces, if necessary. From within the metric system, convert *grams* to pennyweight or troy ounces also.

You *can convert more directly* than my formulas allow. Unfortunately, it requires the memorization of more obscure numbers. I added a step to the formulas instead of introducing new numbers. This method helped me memorize more quickly with less mental clutter.

CONVERT "LB, OZ" TO OZ

Where "a" equals total ounces	**(lb × 16) + oz = a**
Scale reads "4lb, 6oz".	
Multiply the number of pounds by 16 to convert pounds to ounces.	4 × 16
Add the remaining ounces to that product.	(4 × 16) + 6
The converted weight is 70 ounces.	(4 × 16) + 6 = 70

Table 9.2

Convert Oz to Dwt

Where "b" equals total pennyweights	**(oz × 28.35) × .64 = b**
Scale reads "8.24oz".	
Multiply the number of ounces by 28.35 to convert ounces to grams.	8.24 × 28.35
Multiply that product by .64 to convert grams to pennyweights.	(8.24 × 28.35) × .64
The converted weight is 149.5 pennyweights.	(8.24 × 28.35) × .64 = 149.5

Table 9.3

Convert Oz to Ozt

Where "c" equals total troy ounces	**(oz × 28.35) / 31.1 = c**
Scale reads "88.24oz".	
Multiply the number of ounces by 28.35 to convert ounces to grams.	88.24 × 28.35
Divide that product by 31.1 to convert grams to troy ounces.	(88.24 × 28.35) / 31.1
The converted weight is 80.43 troy ounces.	(88.24 × 28.35) / 31.1 = 80.43

Table 9.4

Covert G to Dwt

Where "b" equals total pennyweights	**g × .64 = b**
Scale reads "8.2g".	
Multiply the number of grams by .64 to convert grams to pennyweights.	8.2 × .64
The converted weight is 5.2 pennyweights.	8.2 × .64 = 5.2

Table 9.5

Convert G to Ozt

Where "c" equals total troy ounces	**(g × .64) / 20 = c**
Scale reads "88.2g"	
Multiply the number of grams by .64 to convert grams to pennyweights.	88.2 × .64
Divide that product by 20 to convert pennyweights to troy ounces.	(88.2 × .64) / 20
The converted weight is 2.8 troy ounces.	(88.2 × .64) / 20 = 2.8

Table 9.6

Daily Rates and Formulas Overview

A successful gold buyer knows two things at all times. First, he follows spot prices like a stockbroker watches stocks. When they move, he sees it. Second, he maintains updated buy prices (the amounts that he pays) for 10K, 14K, and 18K gold and sterling silver. This is standard practice since buyers encounter these materials most often. Additionally, he can calculate other prices (i.e., bullion or 22K gold) expeditiously.

He checks spot prices at the beginning of each workday. With those numbers he calculates his basic buying prices ahead of business activities. He will use those same spot values to calculate other prices when necessary. During *volatile* periods he checks the COMEX *continually* and adjusts his numbers accordingly.

Typically, buyers figure scrap prices per pennyweight of gold and per troy ounce of silver. Prices for bullion depend on the weight of each item. US junk silver prices are calculated per $1 of face value. Other countries calculate according to standard denominations of their coinage See Appendix B for the details.

The next few sections examine specific formulas for calculating value. You will use these to valuate every item or load you purchase. I have assumed some numbers for demonstration purposes. You can specify the variables later. In other words, replace my numbers with the correct spot (in your national currency), purity, rate or cut, etc.

SPP

"SPP" is one of my personal nomenclatures—not common terminology. SPP stands for "Spot Price Per". It expresses spot values for standard measurements of specific metal varieties. Is that too confusing? COMEX states a spot price for one *troy ounce* of *pure* gold. The SPP equation can derive the value for one *pennyweight* of *14K* gold.

The SPP formula is of little significance by itself. Rather, consider it is a mathematical landmark. It is the starting point on an algebraic path to your purchase price. It is a root of other equations—the y just add steps to it. So learning to find SPP helps you remember the routes to other answers.

Gold SPP

Type	Spot	Purity	(Spot × Purity / 20) = SPP dwt
10K	$900	.4166	(900 × .4166 / 20) = $18.74
14K	$900	.583	(900 × .583 / 20) = $26.23
18K	$900	.75	(900 × .75 / 20) = $33.75

Table 9.7

Silver SPP

Type	Spot	Purity	(Spot × Purity) = SPP ozt
Sterling	$15	.925	(15 × .925) = $13.87

Table 9.8

BPP

BPP, or "Buying Price Per", is another of my simplistic inventions. Every SPP has a BPP counterpart. SPP specifies spot value; BPP denotes what you pay.

Round down each BPP to the nearest quarter. Substitute a similar denomination if you're outside of the United States. Rounding makes the values easier to remember and work with throughout your day. Rounding *down* prevents your estimation from costing you. Round up only if the number falls at the edge of a higher amount. For example, round $15.24 up a penny to $15.25 (instead of rounding down 24 cents).

At appointments, just multiply each part of the load by its respective BPP. For example, multiply 14K gold weight by 14K BPP. Then add up the subtotals to determine your total buying price for the load. Starting at BPP saves you from running through the entire equation repeatedly. It is shorthand. Thus knowing your BPPs improves your efficiency.

There are two basic methods for calculating your buy prices. I will refer to them as the Rate Method and Cut Method. The Rate Method *multiplies SPP by a percentage of spot*. The Cut Method *subtracts a cut or commission from SPP*. Nothing restricts you exclusively to either method. The difference between SPP and BPP is your profit margin.

I favored the Rate Method. By now you understand that precious metal prices change constantly. Technically, there is no way to guarantee the same *prices* to every client. So this method enabled me to guarantee the same *rates*.

These two methods differ by a single step. We'll avoid the redundancy of presenting two complete versions of every formula below. I will show you the Rate Method. You can change these formulas into the Cut Method by editing one step. Just replace the rate multiplier with a subtraction step. It's easier to demonstrate math than to discuss it. So the first equation includes such an example.

What percentage of spot will you pay customers? What commission will you charge? The answers depend upon your pricing strategy and operating costs. My obvious costs included gas, supplies, marketing materials, shipping, refinery fees, and a cell phone. Income taxes took the biggest bite of all.

Other costs are hidden. Sometimes prices drop before you can lock in. Some pieces turn out to be bogus or of lower karat than you expected. A successful gold buyer covers all costs and still produces a pleasurable profit.

Look through your phone book or search online for local buyers. Call them as a customer. Ask about their gold and silver buy prices. Calculate what percentage of the market value that equates to.[$] Set your prices a little higher, if possible. Keep in mind this method serves as an approximation only. Some buyers will quote one price on the phone but finagle the numbers at their appointments.

[$] Divide the quoted price by the appropriate SPP to determine the rate of spot. If the buyer says he pays $25 per pennyweight of 14K gold. Divide $25 by the SPP for 14K gold. The result is his rate.

Gold BPP (Rate Method)

Type	Spot	Purity	Rate	(Spot × Purity / 20) × Rate = BPP
10K	$900	.4166	70%	(900 × .4166 / 20) × .65 = $13.12[$]
14K	$900	.583	70%	(900 × .583 / 20) × .65 = $18.36
18K	$900	.75	70%	(900 × .75 / 20) × .65 = $23.62

Table 9.9

Gold BPP (Cut Method)[$]

Type	Spot	Purity	Cut	(Spot × Purity / 20) – Cut = BPP
10K	$900	.4166	$5.50	(900 × .4166 / 20) – 5.5 = $13.24
14K	$900	.583	$8.00	(900 × .583 / 20) – 8 = $18.23
18K	$900	.75	$10.25	(900 × .75 / 20) – 10.25 = $23.50

Table 9.10

Silver BPP

Type	Spot	Purity	Rate	(Spot × Purity) × Rate = BPP
Sterling	$15	.925	60%	(15 × .925) × .60 = $8.32

Table 9.11

[$] Remember to round down your BPPs to the nearest quarter. For example, you would round down to $13 for your 10K BPP.
[$] The Cut Method replaces "x Rate" (in the Rate Method) with "- Cut".

Bullion and Junk Silver Specifics

Pricing bullion and coins is different from pricing scrap: it usually doesn't even require a calculator. Just call your refinery when you come across these items. Better yet, contact the refinery ahead of meeting any caller who *mentions* bullion or coins. Ask the refinery's price. Subtract a commission; the remainder is your buying price. In this case the Cut Method is the easiest option.

If the refinery pays $900 per troy ounce of .999 gold, then you pay $850 per ozt. If the refinery pays 8 times face for 90% silver coins, pay 6.5 times face. You can do this whether or not you actually sell these items to the refinery.

What if you can't reach the refinery at the exact moment you need a price, though? Then you will need a formula to fall back on. Both bullion and junk silver require unique considerations.

Bullion is pure. Therefore, we don't multiply spot by purity to find SPP. Essentially, spot *is* SPP for bullion. So we find bullion BPP differently than for other items. Gold bullion also comes in gram weights. So this requires a second formula which incorporates metric conversion.

You don't *weigh* silver coins; you *count* them. Junk silver BPP figures upon a basic unit of currency. For example, buyers figure US coin prices per $1 of face value. Every $1 face value combination of US 90% silver (except Morgan and Peace dollars) contains the same amount (.725 ozt) of pure silver. Four quarters contain .725 ozt of pure silver; so do ten dimes.

This principle also applies to other US and world junk silver varieties. For instance, one British crown features the same silver content as five shillings. Use the details from Appendix B, along with the equation below, to calculate your junk silver BPPs.

Your will enjoy a larger profit margin on gold and silver scrap than on other items. Buyers pay proportionately more for bullion and coins. The reason: clients can compare prices on these items easily. They don't need special scales and intimate knowledge of measurements. They can call any dealer and ask for price quotes. However, you will learn how to sell these items at a premium (Chapter 13).

BPP must be multiplied by something in order to yield a total price. In the case of scrap gold or silver, you multiply it by load weight. For bullion or coins you substitute content or face value, respectively. Different categories of items require different multipliers:

- ✓ Multiply gold bullion BPP by .10 for a $^{1}/_{10}{}^{th}$ ozt Gold Eagle.
- ✓ Multiply silver bullion BPP by 15 for 15 ozt of silver bullion.
- ✓ Multiply metric BPP by 5 for a 5g gold ingot.
- ✓ Multiply 90% junk silver BPP by the total face value of 90% silver coins.

BULLION BPP (GOLD AND SILVER)

Spot	Rate	Spot × Rate = BPP ozt
$900	85%	900 × .85 = $765
$15	85%	15 ×.85 = $12.75

Table 9.12

BULLION BPP (METRIC)

Spot	Rate	Spot / 31.1 × Rate = BPP g
$900	85%	900 / 31.1 × .85 = $24.59

Table 9.13

JUNK SILVER BPP (US 90%)

Spot	Content	Rate	Spot × Content × Rate = BPP $1 face
$15	.715 ozt	75%	15 × .715 × .75 = $8.04

Table 9.14

War nickels hardly qualify as junk silver. Many refineries pay but a fraction of their silver value.[$] Furthermore, I bet you will see fewer of them than other silver coins. Nobody ever sold me a bag of silver nickels. When I occasionally found them, it was always among a pile of worthless coins. Nevertheless, you can create a pricing formula for them. Base it on the standard junk silver equation.

Ask your refinery what *percentage* of spot they pay for silver nickels. Convert the percentage to a decimal. Then insert it ("RRate") in the equation between "Content" and "Rate". To profit you must pay less than the refinery's rate. The silver content of war nickels is 1.125 ozt per dollar of face value.

WAR NICKEL BPP

Spot	Content	RRate	Rate	Spot × Content × RRate × Rate = BPP $1 face
$15	1.125 ozt	?	75%	15 × 1.125 × ? × .75 = ?

Table 9.15

[$] War nickels contain a 9% manganese alloy which complicates and increases the cost of the silver extraction.

Exercise

Imagine sitting at your client's table. You have checked everything with a magnet, examined for markings, tested, and weighed. Now find your total price for the client's items:

- ★ 12.7 dwt of 14K gold jewelry
- ★ 44.6 oz. of sterling silverware
- ★ 1 (one) 1/4 ozt Gold Eagle
- ★ 16 (sixteen) 1964 silver quarters

Use your BPPs, and convert measurements. Then add it all together. You will pay $775[$]; just follow these steps.

1. $18.25 × 12.7 = $216
2. (44.6 × 28.35) / 31.1 = 40.65 ozt, *and then* $8.25 × 40.65 = $338
3. $765 × .25 = $191
4. $8 × 4 = $32
5. $216 + $338 + $191 + $32 = $777

[$] See page 136 for explanation.

The End

As you figure each pile's value jot the totals in a notebook. This is your safety net. Calculating these numbers can be a simple task. On the other hand, trying to remember some numbers, while still calculating others, is nearly impossible. Moreover, it is unnecessary.

Scribble your totals inconspicuously. Be casual but intentional. Don't slap your hand over your notes and eagle eye clients to see if they're peeking. Just try to avoid their seeing your notes. Write small, or close the notebook between entries; excessive openness prompts intrusive questions. Your procedural considerations and adjustments are irrelevant. Your *final price* is all that customers *need* to know.

Make any necessary adjustments before announcing your grand total. For small loads, round down enough to glean a worthwhile profit. Round up on large loads to pay a little extra in exchange for the large volume. What if you doubt the authenticity or actual purity of some items? Factor in an allowance to compensate your risk. Conversely, don't buy those items. Choose quickly. Then pay up; your customer is waiting

CHAPTER 10

Virtual Training: A Workday Walk-thru

A Typical Scenario

It's Monday morning, and you are setting up for work. First, you check spot prices and calculate BPPs. Spot didn't change over the weekend; markets were closed. There was some volatility at the end of last week, though. When that happens, you always expect price settling as markets reopen.

You check your email inbox. A potential customer wrote to you with questions. You reply thoughtfully and begin preparing for today's business. So far, you have a noon appointment across town.

Your cell phone rings. The caller wants to sell a few gold necklaces and asks about your service. You recite your usual quick explanation and offer to set an appointment. He accepts. So, you ask for his particulars and schedule him after your noon meeting. Next use MapQuest, Googlemaps, or a GPS to pinpoint his address and plot a route to both appointments.

Your briefcase is packed; your gas tank is full. Check that you have sufficient cash and different denominations. You need enough of both to pay multiple customers.

You arrive at your appointment with supplies in hand. Your appearance and conduct both assert, "Professional". The client answers her door; you introduce yourself with a handshake. She invites you in and shows you where to sit.

Her items are waiting on the table already. Otherwise, she will bring them to you. Ask her to turn on another light, if necessary; you need to see everything clearly. Pull out your loupe, magnet, test kit, calculator, and notepad.

Put clients at ease. Most of them are guarded even if willing to meet with you. Be relaxed and confident. Now is a good time to ask her some questions:

- **?** Do you have other jewelry, coins, or silverware you would consider selling?
- **?** How did you find out about me?
- **?** What search terms did you use?$
- **?** Do you have any feedback about my advertising?
- **?** Did you contact or consider contacting any other buyers?

$ Ask this only if the client found you through an online search.

She will probably ask you some standard questions too. So have your with your standard answers ready. It isn't an act, but it is a routine. Clients ask the same questions:

? How did you get into this business?

? What do you do with the stuff you buy?

? What percentage of value are you paying me?

? How many pennyweights are in an ounce?[$]

? Do you pay more than other buyers?

? What would another buyer pay me?

? What do my items weigh?

? Why do you need my ID?

? Do you pay for gemstones?

? Do you pay for *really nice* gemstones?

? Can you remove my gemstones for me?

[$] If you mention "pennyweight", some customers seek further explanation.

Most customers enjoy a good conversation. They share a lot of interesting stories, and commonalities emerge. For instance, one of my frequent clients was born in my hometown 800-miles away. Furthermore, every customer interaction is a chance to improve your business. Knowing your audience helps you market properly. Pause and ask for a quiet minute when you need to count coins or calculate numbers.

Follow proper procedures. Float your magnet over the items first. Remove those that stick. Next inform your client that testing involves scratching or filing the pieces. Secure permission and then test the uncertain pieces. Continually remove those that fail testing, and sort those that pass. When finished, weigh everything and calculate total value. Did you yet ask if she has any other items to sell?

If nothing else, *ask every client for other items*. She may not realize that you purchase jewelry *and* silverware *and* coins. My ads were clear, but, for some reason, customers were not. More than one customer exclaimed to me, "Oh I didn't know you buy that too." On the other hand, she may have held a few items back. Nonetheless, your unassuming question will convince her to retrieve them. This is referred to as an "upsell" in marketing terminology. You upsell by persuading the customer to increase the current transaction.

Declare your price. She will likely accept your offer. She might ask a question or two but will not resist if you seem trustworthy and sincere. If her friend referred her to you, that also increases your credibility.

Ask for her photo ID and fill out a receipt. Collect the metal in baggies and stow your tools. Pay her in cash as soon as she signs the receipt. Thank her and hand her a few business cards for friends and family. Request her recommendation if she was happy with your service.

Solicit referrals after each successful transaction. Some clients would automatically tell their friends. Surprisingly, that idea wouldn't occur to others at all. *Ask* for referrals while *informing* them that you receive a lot of referrals. Referrals are free and extremely effective publicity; take full advantage of them.

Continue to your next appointment and so on. Add the day's acquisitions to your stash when you return home. Subsequently, record all your purchases in your ledger. My final task each day was hand writing "Thank You" post cards. I mailed them the next day on the way to other appointments.

Monitor the size of your load. Call your refinery to lock in for an assay when you accumulate enough weight. Then prepare your package and mail it, or drive it to the refinery. Your check should arrive in 2 weeks or less.

Email Inquiries

Typically, parties who contact you by email are less committed than callers. Email is a no-pressure way to ask questions without answering any. In my experience, email inquiries were equivalent to store browsing. Convinced clients called and requested appointments.

Reply to emails thoughtfully. Thank people for contacting you, and answer their questions. Some people email about a pair of gold earrings or silver plated flatware. Invite them to contact you again if they find more items or know somebody who needs your service. Encourage the rest to call you to set appointments.

Don't use sentence fragments or give one-line replies: nobody likes that. You want to reel in customers not save time with sloppy emails. Email is another marketing tool. Lazy email responses show customers a lack of courtesy and interest.

Some contacts, if you let them, would email you numerous times with many questions but no intention of calling. I don't know why; it doesn't really matter. Those who *will* call typically do so after your first or second reply.

This pattern taught me to recognize window shoppers. I set a limit and stopped answering questions after two responses. From that point on, I only advised a call. That way, the person either called or stopped writing.

Phone Inquiries

The original call is your ripest opportunity to schedule a client. This is not always possible, though. For instance, you could be busy with another customer at that moment. In that case, ask for the caller's name and address. Promise to call back as soon as possible; offer a time frame. Next check your availability and the caller's location. Call back when you can with an open time slot in mind.

Buyer, beware. A phone call is the closest you will get to a customer before meeting. Turn on the radar; listen for hints of trouble. It is easier to avoid danger than to escape it. You are not obligated to anything. Infrequently, when callers raised my suspicions, I declined them appointments.$

Selecting a Meeting Place

Some callers are uncomfortable with house visits. They don't mind the landscaper or the cleaning service coming out. Ironically, they think twice about the gold buyer: he's a *stranger*. Don't take it personally. It is wise for them to be wary. However, since they called you, they probably want to deal.

Assuage their uneasiness with reassurance and a workaround solution. Offer to meet at a coffee shop or in a parking lot. Bear in mind that some stores maintain policies against outside operators. An employee may ask you to leave if somebody sees you conducting business. So avoid making a spectacle, or go to a park instead.

Scheduling

Set approximate times for appointments. Scheduling is an art—not a science. You may be delayed or arrive early. Usually, neither is a problem as long as you notify the

$ Consider also taking proactive steps to avoid problems. I steered clear of high crime areas, and my advertising displayed my stance against illegal activities.

customer. Say, for example, "I'll see you around 1:30—give or take 20 minutes."

Ask what your caller wants to sell. This helps you estimate appointment length. A few rings require less time than a bunch of jewelry and coins. Bear in mind, though, that your customer may forget to mention something. Similarly, an upsell would result in more merchandise to process. Thus you can never know exactly how long an appointment will take until you get there.

Let's say you receive a call from a nearby seller during an appointment. You want to meet that customer before driving to the next scheduled appointment. If you expect to be late, always call your next client as soon as you can guess how late.

Consolidate appointments; it spares your time and money. Imagine you have three prospective clients, and two are in the same area. Try to schedule all three during the same part of the day. Furthermore, schedule appointments consecutively that are near each other. Attempt to finish in one area before traveling to another.

Why Some Clients Refuse to Sell

What happened? The client called. You answered his questions and set an appointment. Then you spent valuable time driving to him and examining his items. You even offered a good price! So why did he not sell to you?

This situation is anticlimactic but inevitable. Don't let it bother you. Around 1 in 15 of my appointments ended this way; that's business. No store sells to 100% of its visitors. Likewise, even successful gold buyers experience occasional letdowns. I modeled my business to give customers *every* reason to sell to Metal Man. Yet one particular obstruction prevented some from seeing that—unrealistic expectation.

The client hoped for a certain price, but that price was inflated. He based his estimate on daydreams or assumptions—not facts. By so doing, he prematurely fixed his mind on an inaccurate number. My solid offer seemed meager in comparison. Unrealistic expectations stem from a few common mistakes:

- The client is relying too heavily on the original purchase price.
- The client is biased by sentimental value.
- The client needs a specific amount of money and convinces himself that his items are worth that amount.
- The client does not sufficiently understand spot, purity, or measurements.[$]

Explain the mistake clearly and diplomatically. Some customers will see the sense in it. Unfortunately, others

---

[$] For example, the client heard on the radio that gold was worth $900 per ounce. Then he weighed his 14K items at the post office. They totaled 2 ounces (not troy ounces). So he expected $1800 from you.

won't believe you. They will assume your explanation is a last ditch effort to reach into their pockets. Oh well.

Similarly, some ambivalent customers ask about a second visit. "Will you come back if I decide to sell later?" they wonder aloud. In the beginning, hungry for business, I agreed to this option. Then I realized they rarely called back afterward. It showed me that my initial visit was my best chance to buy.

So I adopted a "now or never" policy. My amended response to this question left the client no wiggle room. "Market prices change. So this is my price right now. I spent enough time here already, and I have other clients to meet." Sometimes this ultimatum tipped the scale in my favor. Some clients just need that extra push.

Paying

Be careful with your money. Specifically, take precautions when counting a customer's payout. Count it under the table or behind the open lid of your briefcase. Customers should focus on the money you give them rather than how much is left in your pocket.

Paying odd dollar amounts requires carrying too many $1 bills. So I always rounded down to the nearest $5 mark. (Choose your own denomination when dealing in other currencies.) That is why you paid $775, instead of $777, in Chapter 9.

Always pay clients with the biggest bills possible. Big bills save space in your pocket. They also make a strong impression. Customers feel like they hit the jackpot when they see Franklin and Grant (or Queen Elizabeth) smiling (sort of) back at them.

I carried my money in separate pockets: $100 bills in one and smaller bills in the other. Here's how I would pay $775 to the customer. I reach into my first pocket and pull out seven bills only. I don't need to remove the whole fold and look at it; because *all the bills are hundreds.* Next I discreetly take the bills from my second pocket. Removing a $50, $20, and $5 bill from an organized fold is quick and easy. That's it—no fumbling or flipping through a huge wad of cash while drawing green-eyed stares.

CHAPTER 11

EXPOSE YOURSELF, PART I: ADVERTISING

As a budding entrepreneur I needed effective marketing methods. I read a book, *Guerilla Marketing,* by Jay Conrad Levinson. It was an excellent study of strategic shoestring marketing.

Small businesses cannot compete with big business budgets. However, they *can* focus sharply on niche markets. Then they can market to their audiences less expensively and more efficiently. I attribute much of my marketing paradigm to Mr. Levinson's book.

The action of marketing is composed of two activities—advertising and promotion. Advertising tells people who you are and what you do. Promotion incentivizes people to deal with you. Through trial and error I crafted a successful marketing plan. The following ideas paid huge dividends for me.

Message

Your marketing message is your main attraction. You can advertise all day long, but advertising alone doesn't generate customers. You need a motivating message to make your phone ring.

Be clear, concise, and deliberate in your advertising. Write ad copy with buzz words like "cash", "fast", "quick", and "easy". Replace boring statements with positive action phrases (Table 11.1). Assert the benefits of your service: who needs it, and why? Explain your competitive advantages. Why should sellers choose you over other buyers? Lastly, consistency is your ally. Don't change your message unless it doesn't work or stops working.

All your ads and marketing materials should express the same message. In so doing, they will reinforce each other. Repeat your slogan and key points, therefore. The sentence you read twice lingers longer than two different sentences. The sentence you read twice lingers longer than two different sentences. Repetition resonates and fosters familiarity.

Themed marketing creates visual recognition for you. Let's say I just started a new job in a crowded corporate environment. Everybody looks the same. Though I blend in with common attire, *some* people will recognize me . . . eventually, *hopefully*. On the other hand, what if I wear the same red shirt and blue pants every day?

Soon I'm not just another face; I am the guy in the red shirt and blue pants. People now notice me who would never notice me otherwise. They begin wondering, "What's up with that guy in the red shirt and blue pants?" Suddenly I seem to be everywhere—in the hallway, the elevator, and the cafeteria lunch line. In reality, they just recognize me wherever I go. My "marketing plan" brought me out of obscurity into the spotlight. Consequently, more people will notice me more quickly and more often than before.

Each of Metal Man's marketing materials incorporated the same backgrounds and colors. My business cards and magnets were nearly identical. The brochures were similar but more descriptive and illustrative. Furthermore, they all stated the same points in the same way. Even my website repeated all of this but gave greater detail. The word to remember is "synergy"; you want all your efforts to work together towards success.

Positive Action Phrases

Boring	Better
"Gold is worth money."	"Get cash for your gold." "Sell your gold for cash." "Metal Man will buy your gold." "Metal Man pays you cash for gold."
"I offer high prices."	"I pay you more." "I pay the most cash." "We pay you the most cash for your gold."
"Phone: 555-1234"	"Call Now! 555-1234" "CALL NOW! 555-1234"

Table 11.1

Business Cards

A successful gold buyer carries business cards at all times. Think of them as small, inexpensive ads. Disperse them liberally. Use them to reinforce personal encounters. I handed out three cards at a time to clients and contacts. I requested that they share the extra cards with friends.

Leave cards behind you, like footprints, wherever you go. Include these little billboards with your waitress's tip. Ask businesses if you can place a small stack on their checkout counters. A business card is a versatile advertising tool. You would have no excuse whatsoever to be without them.

The next worst thing to not having cards is having dull cards. Business cards are ubiquitous. Yours should stand out from the rest. Lifeless, nondescript cards may present the same information as creative cards. Yet they won't project the same image or effect the same impression. A plain white card with black type represents wasted opportunity.

A good card displays your name, logo, poignant slogan, and contact information. It *grabs* attention. Forget the boring black stock image; you can take advantage of infinite design possibilities. You only create a slogan and logo once, so put some effort into them.

I found Vistaprint before starting Metal Man. They quickly became my prized source for all marketing materials. They offer many colorful and creative stock templates. They can help you craft your own product from scratch too. You can make two-sided cards, add your own images, and even impose backgrounds. Occasionally I called them for professional assistance. They charged just $5 for live service, no matter how long they helped.

The first step with Vistaprint is to open an account. It requires only an email address and password. Your products and orders stay on file in your account. This makes future work a cinch. After your first order you can simply reorder the same products. Furthermore, you can edit or entirely redesign them online anytime.

Vistaprint prices are the lowest, or among the lowest, around. Still, you can pay even less by taking advantage of regular discounts. Visit *www.vistaprint.com* and sign up for their promotional emails. Don't order anything; just sign up.

Soon you will begin receiving frequent offers of huge savings on their products. Purchase your materials using the links and coupon codes they send.

Their online checkout system walks you through the purchase process. This includes a series of advertisements. Decline the ads, but keep your eyes open for the upsell. Just before completing your order they will offer a few more items at substantial discounts.

Let's say you order a thousand business cards. They may offer you a thousand more for an extra few dollars. So always proceed through checkout with a smaller amount of product than you actually want. Wait to see if they offer the upsell. A thousand cards on sale costs little. However, five hundred cards on sale plus another five hundred at upsell price costs even less. If they don't offer what you want, simply amend your order just before paying.

Follow-up Materials

I mailed post cards to each new customer following our first successful transaction. I copied their addresses from my receipts. The front side featured my business name, contact details, and slogan. The focal point: a striking image of a handshake portrayed under a prominent "Thank You."

The back side presented a handwritten message (as shown by Figure E). I *could have* ordered my post cards pre-printed with my desired message. It would have cost nearly nothing and saved time. It also would have saved the postcards I goofed up. Nonetheless, handwritten messages are more personal and endearing.

These cards performed multiple duties. First, they demonstrated gratefulness to clients. Businesses depend on customers. So I wanted customers to feel appreciated, even *after* transactions. Secondly, some sellers might wonder if they had been scammed. The "Thank You" cards could salve lingering suspicion. Scammers typically don't consider such gestures. Finally, they reminded clients about our encounter and solicited referrals. Thus they fostered repeat business and word-of-mouth advertising.

SAMPLE POST CARD MESSAGE

Jane,

Thanks for choosing Metal Man as your gold and silver buyer. I hope you were satisfied with the service. If so, please recommend me to others. Contact me anytime.

God bless.

- Metal Man

Figure E

Online Classifieds

Search free classified ad websites in your city. Try "free online classifieds Anycity."[$] Craigslist is the most popular of these sites. Your search will reveal others too if you live in a metropolitan area. Some sites are second-rate: error-ridden or difficult to navigate. Others will prove valuable. Free or low cost online classified posts are an ideal advertising format.

First you register on the site. Then you post a short ad for your service (or product, if you are selling an item). Be sure to post in the designated section (ex. "want to buy" or "jewelry for sale"). Some sites allow you to post daily. Others allow only one post per person, item, category, or week. Read each site's terms of use. The good sites are monitored and will remove posts or ban users who break their rules.

Since Craigslist is the category leader, most people don't bother browsing other sites. Fortunately, your ads reach beyond site-specific visitors. Many ad sites share their listings with search engines. Therefore, prospective clients will discover you during their online searches.

For example, a local person searches for "buy gold Anycity". Meanwhile, your posted ads contain the phrase, "I buy gold in Anycity." The presence of these keywords causes your ads to appear in the search results. Then the person clicks on a search result which connects them to your ad. At that point, he is one step away from contacting you.

[$] Substitute the name of your city in place of "Anycity".

Load your online ads with key words and key phrases. Google offers a keyword tool to help you select the right ammunition.[$] The tool accesses a database of all Google searches performed by users. Enter a word like "gold". It shows how many monthly searches are performed for "gold". It also shows phrases that include "gold" and their monthly search tallies. It can even offer suggestions for relevant phrases. With it you can target your audience through search results. Start by looking for the following keywords and phrases:

- "Gold";
- "Coins";
- "Cash for gold";
- "Buy gold Anycity".

Investigate whether your ads will expire; repost when they do. I posted new ads weekly or monthly, depending on the site rules. Meanwhile, I removed the previous ads only when required. Search engines can take a couple of weeks to locate your ads. So ads may never show up in search results if you remove them too soon.

[$] Visit *www.adwords.google.com/select/KeywordToolExternal* for more information.

Workplaces

I met one client in a national corporate headquarters high-rise. She was impressed with the price I paid for her items. As it turned out, her help profited me more than her gold. The reason: she was the vice president of some department there.

She informed me that her company maintained a computerized bulletin board. There, employees posted "for sale" and "wanted" ads. It circulated weekly on all network computers. She invited me to write an ad for it. At least several hundred people worked there. So that was an excellent opportunity to reach a captive audience.

She reposted my ad every week thereafter. Sure enough, other people in that building soon began calling. Frequently I met with multiple clients per visit. Eventually the employee referrals lent credence to the board posts. Together they perpetuated my unofficial but close relationship with that company.

Old-fashioned bulletin boards work too. They display ads and business cards for passersby to see. You can find them in retirement communities, hospitals, clubhouses, and meeting places. Contact somebody in charge before tacking up your material. That can help ensure your ads remain in place.

Website

Websites are like business cards—every professional should have one. They perform a similar function but with greater detail. Plus, they reach a larger audience through technology than you can by only personal contact. A website's main aim is to explain four things in detail:

- Who you are
- What you do
- Why people should deal with you
- How people can contact you

Unquestionably, my website was one of my most effective marketing tools. The site consisted of only five pages. Along with a homepage it featured pages for FAQs, media items, testimonials, and links. Some visitors found it through search results. Others proceeded there directly from a business card or advertisement.

Together the different pages formed a sales presentation. It expressed my business philosophy and explained my service. Pictures of the items I wanted to buy surrounded the text. It answered common questions and presented real testimonials. It highlighted newspaper articles written about Metal Man. My chamber of commerce member emblem adorned every page. The site communicated that Metal Man was a reputable business. Ultimately, that convinced visitors to contact me.

Creating a website seems intimidating if you know nothing about it. Yet most people can design a decent website with little or no outside help. You don't need to spend a lot of money or hire professionals, though you can. Various programs make it easier than ever before.

A plethora of web hosts vie for your patronage. I have either researched or dealt with most of them. I recommend Go Daddy web hosting. In fact, I chose them to host *www.beagoldbuyer.com!*

Go Daddy is one of the largest companies in the business. They combine excellent security and customer service with outstanding prices. Go Daddy also offers a great tool for building a site–Website Tonight. These are the factors to consider when comparing different web hosts.

You don't need to know complicated html. WYSIWYG site building tools allow you to create a website using "drag and drop" technology.[$] This means you simply move pictures and words wherever you want them on the screen.

Pre-made templates further streamline the process. These offer you an alternative to building your site from scratch. Essentially, just apply the templates and choose your preferences (colors, etc.). Then fill in the blank areas with your own words and images. Go Daddy offers a wide assortment of stock images too.

$ "WYSIWYG" stands for "What You See Is What You Get". Such programs offer a visual site building alternative to html coding.

You can set up quickly with Go Daddy. Furthermore, it probably costs less than you expect. Your domain name will cost $10–$20 depending on your extension (.com, .org, etc.) and add-ons. Another $6–$10 per month will pay for your hosting. The profit potential of a good website dwarfs its measly cost. Visit *www.godaddy.com* for more information.

Outside programs can increase your design options. I use WYSIWYG Web Builder 7 to create my sites. It affords creative freedom far beyond Website Tonight templates. It pairs a full feature set with ease of use. I have also found it to be stable and dependable where other programs have failed. Moreover, the support is unmatched. Post a question anytime; the forum is filled with eager respondents. Visit *www.wysiwygwebbuilder.com* to learn more.

Merchandise

How many of your pens are labeled with business names? I have a drawer full of them. The problem: I never look at the pens when I write; I only look at what I'm writing. Therefore, each pen exemplifies misspent money by a company. I don't care if every business gives out free pens. They only waste money if they don't generate customers.

Carefully chosen merchandise *can* market for you effectively, though. You don't even need to offer free clothing, mugs, or pogo sticks. You run a business—not a charity. You distribute *inexpensive* merchandise solely as a means to advertise. People take it because they like freebies. Each taker is, potentially, an affordable commercial for you.

As a gold buyer I gave out magnets—three per customer. Do magnets seem as worthless as pens? These weren't. My magnets mirrored the front of my business cards. They were the same size and shape and bore the same design. Consequently, they built brand recognition. They also elicited many compliments which, again, told me they made the desired impression.

People *use* magnets; they are not destined for desk drawers like pens. Magnets stick to refrigerators and filing cabinets. They don't vanish under car seats. They secure shopping lists, photos, and preschoolers' finger-painted masterpieces in plain sight. They also don't break or dry up. Visitors to a home or office may ask about a magnet that catches their eyes. Magnets fill valuable ad space and are viewed daily.

Imagine two people sitting in a kitchen. One mentions selling gold. The other exclaims, "I know just the guy. I don't need to search for his card, because his information is right here on this magnet." You are the closest gold buyer to every person with your magnet. That is, *unless* she is wearing a shirt, drinking from a mug, or jumping on a pogo stick from another buyer. Fortunately, those chances are slim.

Look at different options. I chose magnets because they were cheap and useful. They also paired well with my high scoring business cards. They worked hard for me, but other products might fit your business better.

Branders secures my recommendation as the best merchandiser. They supply small time operators and large, well-known companies alike. They offer unbeatable prices and even free samples for inspection. Visit *www.branders.com* for details.

Community Involvement

Metal Man targeted an upper middle class suburb just outside the city. Its residents were community-oriented. They preferred to patronize local businesses rather than outsiders. This was one of the main reasons I joined their Chamber of Commerce. Eventually, I also thought to sponsor a little league team.

The overseeing organization charged approximately $250 for team sponsorship. That seemed shockingly low for such positive exposure. I could have pulled $250 out of my sofa by then.

I imagined a bunch of junior athletes suited in Metal Man uniforms. I envisioned buying pizza for the team when they won (although it wasn't required). It would have gratified me personally. Plus the sponsorship would have endeared Metal Man to a lot of parents in a prosperous area.

I discovered the chance mid-season one year. The plan fell through only because I left gold buying prior to the next season. Still, ideas like this deserve your consideration. Investigate similar possibilities like community events or private functions. Good will, affordable advertising, and instant credibility comprise an insuperable marketing combination.

Other Ideas

Advertising is big business. My chamber membership prompted a steady stream of calls from advertisers. They wanted to sell me ad space on gym equipment, in menus, and over urinals (it's true). Those spots might work for some people—but not Metal Man. I knew my customer base and where to find them. I also knew what would contradict my image—like urinal ads.

Knowing your customer is the number one rule of marketing. How can you play darts without seeing the bull's eye? First you must know who you want to reach. Only then can you figure out how to reach them.

Bench backs and bus stops buoy some buyers. Placing brochures in banks would better befit others. The right choice is the method that finds your audience and, in some cases, *only* your audience.

Marketing costs vary as much as the methods. In fact, the real costs can only be measured by results. A television commercial might cost 10 times more than Metal Man pens up front. Yet the pens cost more in real terms if the commercial brings 20 times more customers.

Your most effective methods must focus sharply on your clientele. Otherwise, they should reach a large audience inexpensively. Your marketing dollars are limited. Therefore, you must find out where your clients gather and go there—figuratively and literally. A small business need not spend big advertising dollars.

How can you spread the word about your service? Place an ad in your local penny pincher magazine or community newspaper. Print brochures, and solicit permission to place them at area establishments. Create complimentary company bookmarks; leave them at a library.

The principles of marketing favor creativity; cost is irrelevant to effectiveness. Creative ideas stand out from the rest. If the library allowed them, your bookmarks might enjoy exclusive access. If nobody else thought of them, yours won't be crowded out by other bookmarks. In this way the unique idea grabs the spotlight with a solo appearance. I would rather burn dollar bills for heat than pay a king's ransom for an ad in the yellow pages Try a new thing or try an old thing in a new way.

Search online for articles and merchandise options. There are multitudinous ways to publicize your services. Experiment with different ideas. Track your results to see what works best for you. Keep and improve the productive ideas; discard the rest.

Caution about Advertising

I once considered buying large magnetic signs for my car doors. They would have improved my *visibility,* but visibility is not always beneficial. Sometimes I didn't want to be seen. I certainly didn't want people around me wondering about my pockets' contents. Announcing my presence might have stimulated more than innocent curiosity. The risks outweighed the benefits.

Some marketing methods are inappropriate for gold buyers. In my *opinion,* a boldly labeled uniform is another example. Remember that you carry cash and precious metals. Take your location into account. Anticipate who would be reached by various marketing efforts. Decide what is right for you according to your own criteria.

CHAPTER 12

EXPOSE YOURSELF, PART II: PROMOTION

Warning Statement

My marketing message emphasized what customers could expect from me. Part of it also stipulated my standards for them. The warning statement was a caveat to the main message, but inseparable, nonetheless. All Metal Man ads and materials included it. My website and brochures displayed the full statement (Figure F). Business cards and ads contained a partial declaration, due to limited space.

The statement acted as a deterrent: it clarified my legal stance. So troublemakers didn't bother calling me in the first place. Asking for ID at the transaction was mere formality.

So how does a deterrent promote? Well, honest sellers weren't deterred at all. They *didn't want* an illegitimate gold buyer. It painted Metal Man as a businessman on the up and up rather than some shady character. It implied ethical behavior—the kind of buyer they were looking for. Numerous customers remarked positively about the policy. Thus it was not only preventive but promotional as well.

WARNING STATEMENT

ATTENTION: Metal Man is an honest buyer for honest sellers. We do not take part in illegal or questionable activities. Clients must be of sound and sober mind. No minors. ID required. We do not buy stolen property and will alert authorities to any suspected criminal activity. We may refuse service to anyone at anytime.

Figure F

Guarantee

Retailers offer refunds to pave the way for patrons. These days, stores allow customers to return items for any reason. Shoppers receive money back—no questions asked. This policy removes a mental obstacle to buying. It coaxes the customer toward the purchase. You cannot refund melted metal, though. So what *can* you offer in lieu of it?

Give them a guarantee. Focus it on your strengths and competitive advantages. Promise a quantifiable result such as, “Appointments within 24 hours!” Otherwise, pledge something less tangible like, “Fast service!” My two-sided business cards displayed “The Metal Man Guarantee” on back (Figure G).

Pawnbrokers, jewelers, and by-mail buyers may be among my readers. Please pardon any offense if you are (or hope to become) one of them. This statement was not a personal attack on other gold buyers. Rather it addressed the concerns of my specific audience. Meanwhile it underscored my relative advantages.

I once saw a similar commercial for a jeweler. The narrator warned viewers about inviting "strange buyers" to their homes. He advised bringing their gold to that jeweler as the safer alternative. Of course you can highlight your advantages in like fashion.

THE METAL MAN GUARANTEE

> "The METAL MAN Guarantee"
>
> Avoid the meager payouts and uncertainty of pawn shops, jewelers, web-based, and underground buyers. We are local, legal, and reputable—always ethical, always professional. We come to you and pay more, standard. We respect our customers, value our relationships, and seek to exceed your expectations. We GUARANTEE a fair price—no hassles and no worries. CALL 555-1234 or visit WWW.(removed url).COM for more info!

Figure G

Memberships and Credentials

I pinpointed Metal Man's particular priorities and policies in previous sections. These were birthed from personal convictions. I *learned* to market them as strengths. However, they did not begin as marketing devices. Nor was I originally aiming at a specific audience.

Nonetheless, my brand identity struck a chord with certain sellers. My first two customers, and the majority of the rest, belonged to an easily distinguished demographic. Clients shared similar financial standings and lived in the same general area.

I resided within city limits. A nearby suburb yielded the lion's share of my business. So one of my first clear goals was to establish credibility with that base. After a while, I applied to their Chamber of Commerce rather than my home chamber. It cost just $350 per year and was worth every penny.

The chamber allowed me use of their logo. I plastered it on all my marketing materials. It was better than a BBB (Better Business Bureau) logo for me. It fully validated me to that community. Then the residents considered me a local business and, therefore, a community partner.

The chamber membership included other perks as well. First, they arranged a televised interview through a local station. I still have the DVD copy of it. Second, they listed me on their website along with a detailed description of my service. The listing contained a hotlink which delivered customers directly to my website. Third, they featured my listing in their annual publication of all member businesses. Fourth, they gave my brochures dedicated space in their lobby. Additionally, the chamber organized a multitude of events through which I could promote Metal Man.

My home chamber was prohibitively expensive. I recommend joining your local chamber only if it is affordable. BBB membership can be costly too, although it probably aids credibility. Sometimes their prices overshadow the benefits.

Consider national associations, like Jewelers of America, instead. You can find other groups online by searching for "Anycity jewelers association" or "Anycountry jewelers association". Seek out pawnbroker associations in the same way. Likewise, search for local organizations that repute qualifying businesses. Often, local groups cost less than their regional and national counterparts. They may also tender more relevance with your audience. See Appendix C for more options.

Such organizations offer unique benefits, but alternatives exist. Earn a course certificate in business ethics. Attain a program diploma in gemology or appraising. Study through distance learning while you work. Even unrelated credentials can add distinction. For instance, one gold buyer I knew was also a licensed notary public. Official credits can elevate a gold buyer's public standing.

Special Offers

Special offers from retailers focus on discounts. Yet clients don't *buy* from you; they *sell* to you. Instead of saving their money, your special offers can give them money.

Worthwhile offers should mutually benefit the seller and buyer. The successful gold buyer doesn't mind paying some sellers more. However, he doesn't just throw money away either. Paying extra is a tactical investment, and investors seek returns. Your offers should aim to generate more customers and larger transactions.

Set expiration dates on your offers. These encourage sellers to act now rather than allowing procrastination. You might be willing to extend some offers permanently. Just re-release the coupon with a new expiration date later. Many stores use this same strategy to motivate customers with a sense of urgency. For instance, one footwear chain continually advertises a "buy one pair, pay half price for the second pair" sale. Truly, the sale is perpetual, but their ads always warn, "For a limited time only!"

Set minimum requirements for special offers. Requiring a minimum sale amount ensures adequate profit. The guarantee of a minimum takeaway offsets the smaller profit margin. Sellers don't know their items' values but want to qualify for your offers. Such requirements can compel them to sell everything they are willing to part with. By doing this they hope to meet your minimum.

Display your offers in your marketing materials. Show them on your website. For a fee you can post them on internet coupon sites. Otherwise, you can pay to include them in booklets or mailers. Meanwhile, monitor your bottom line. An offer failed if you only break even after higher payouts and advertising costs.

Metal Man offered 3% extra payout to seniors (age 65 and above) and military veterans. I also posted coupons on the chamber website for free. I remember that one exclaimed, "Receive $10 BONUS on sale of $200 or more!" Consider other ideas too:

🗁 **Bring a friend—both receive 5% BONUS!** I suggest a minimum sale of $250 per person. This will also discourage two people from splitting one person's load in order to use the coupon.

🗁 **3% BONUS on sales over $1000!** Sales like this yield large profits. Moreover, these offers attract wealthy sellers who know other wealthy sellers.

🗁 **$10 BONUS for gold coins!** Require a minimum weight of one troy ounce. This is a great way to gather coins if you need to stock up for resale customers.

🗁 **3% BONUS for selected rings!** You don't want to pay extra for damaged rings. "Selected rings" means rings in resalable condition. The purpose is to bring in quality rings for resale.

🗁 **5% BONUS (over standard 10% commission) for school or other organization fundraisers!** This targets the big business of fundraisers. They can generate large profits you and the organizations involved.[$]

[$] Consider offering half of your profit margin as a standard fundraiser commission. By sweetening the deal, you can attract more fundraisers and motivate their cooperation.

Store coupons provide provable discounts. The customer sees the regular price, uses the coupon, and pays less. The receipt bears evidence of savings. However, contractors' coupons are different.

Once, while a gold buyer, I was looking for contractors to renovate my bathroom. One company offered a coupon for $50 off their normal price. Saving $50 is good. The problem was that the coupon stated, "Must be presented at time of estimate." Instantly my mind imagined a scenario (cue the wavy transition sequence).

I call to invite one of their reps to my home. The guy shows up and looks around. He silently decides the job is $500 worth of work.

Before writing an estimate He asks me, "Do you have any coupons?"

I naively reply, "Why yes. It's right here. It guarantees me fifty bucks off your usual price!"

He recognizes the coupon and agrees, "It *sure* does. . . heh, heh."

Next he calculates some numbers. He signs the estimate form and tears it from his book. He then hands it to me while articulating his explanation.

"This job would have cost you five-hundred and fifty dollars. But you see, sir, I have clearly subtracted your coupon from my usual price. Amazingly, it will only cost you *five-hundred dollars*. When should I start?"

You understand my point here. That coupon leaves too much room for "creative" math. I don't see any honest reason to require the coupon for the estimate. Even if there is a good reason behind it, it doesn't look good to customers.

I didn't want my customers to doubt their discount or suspect me of shenanigans. Therefore, my offers included specific instructions. The coupons directed users to not mention the coupon or discount until *after* I offered my price. Then I would apply it to my stated offer. That way they could know I truly had adjusted their payout.

Sure, even that won't satisfy the most skeptical critics. After all, I *could be* lying about fair pricing. I *could* always calculate a high price first to accommodate expected coupons or haggling. Then the coupon would be a sham.

Still, my offer was unique. It could only be a cleverly devised scheme *or* a thoughtful assurance by an honest buyer. I trusted that, in light of Metal Man's reputation, most people considered it the latter.

Free Publicity

The best source of free local publicity is your local media. Think of something newsworthy about yourself or your business. Write about it, and send it out as a press release. Inform the reader about an event you are organizing, sponsoring, or participating in. Connect your business to current headlines or trends. Otherwise, give them a human interest story concerning your background, circumstances, or customers.

Newspapers, magazines, and television stations are constantly hunting for newsworthy items. You will reap positive exposure if you provide worthwhile content. Another book by Jay Conrad Levinson, *Guerilla Publicity*, provides an enlightening examination of this subject.

I wrote an article for a local newspaper. I titled it, *5 Ways to Save Money Now*. It explained five moneysaving tips. At that time gold was rocketing upwards, and the economy was freefalling. Therefore, the article was timely and relevant.

The article tied in Metal Man at the end. I commented that saving money was great, but that making money was better. Then I extended an invitation to sell me jewelry, coins, and silverware. The invitation specified my contact information and web address. The editor liked the article and ran it right away.

CHAPTER 13

Special Operations: Maximize Your Profit

We covered a lot of ground in the previous chapters. Writing this book has been a huge task for me. There was so much to tell you. By now you know far more than I knew as a beginner. In fact, you know almost everything I ever knew about gold buying. This last chapter will cover the rest. Now let's look at the final few pointers.

Applying all of the revealed information will take practice. In the Army we said, "Slow is smooth; smooth is fast." Take it easy in the beginning. Learn the first steps well before pushing ahead.

Likewise, you should master the *basics* of gold buying first. Memorize the math; try out the tools. Start your business, and spread the word. Gain some experience. Then you can implement the more advanced ideas below.

This last chapter focuses on growing your business. Here we explore strategies to diversify and increase your profitability. I implemented some of these and saw other buyers succeed with the rest.

Gold Parties

Gold parties were the only parties I wanted to attend. Here is how it works. The hostess invites friends to her house. She tells them to bring jewelry because the gold buyer will be there. One by one her guests sell you their items. Afterwards, you pay the hostess a portion of the profits. Then you walk away with a wide smile and bags of gold and silver. Gold parties can be *big time* moneymakers.

Theoretically, men can throw gold parties, but I never saw this. All my gold parties were hosted by women. Therefore, I will use feminine pronouns in this section when referring to the *hostess* and *her* friends.

Advise the hostess to schedule her party in advance. Seven to ten days provides sufficient notice. This allows her friends time enough to plan but not so much as to forget.

Evening is the most popular time of day for gold parties. Clients need adequate time between the end of the workday and the beginning of the party. I scheduled parties around 7 p.m. most often.

The hostess and her friends view the party as a social event. They hang out and chat with each other as if it were a girls' night out. Mid-week parties attract bigger crowds since people make special plans for weekends (including Friday nights).

Some hostesses prefer afternoon appointments instead—when all the kids are at school. During that time, the mothers are unoccupied. Leave this decision up to your hostess's discretion. She knows her guests.

The hostess will introduce you when you arrive. Follow her to your workspace. Organize your area and prepare your tools. Set out a notebook or pad of paper; this will serve as a waiting list. Ask guests to write their names on it. They will mingle while waiting their turns.

Starting with the first name on the list, call the client over. Proceed as you would at any other meeting. Cross her name off the list when you complete the transaction. Subsequently, continue to the second client and so on.

Sometimes, guests leave after you purchase their items. Other times, some or all of them stick around. If any clients remain when you have finished buying, complete your last step quietly.

Review the receipts with your calculator in hand. Tally all of your purchases at that party. You will pay the hostess a commission on those sales.

The promised commission motivated her to organize this shindig in the first place. She operated as a subcontractor of sorts. Her efforts profited you, and she deserves to be compensated accordingly. Obviously, you will not pay a commission on any item the hostess sold you.

I paid my hostesses 10% of the purchases. However, that was not 10% of my profits. Consider the math. Let's say you pay a 65% rate for gold. A 10% commission on that is actually 6.5% of your profits. So in the end you actually pay a 71.5% rate for gold. The rate increase is nullified by the large takeaway, though. The commission is a small business expense to you but a big incentive to the hostess.

Some hostesses sell costume jewelry or cosmetics to their guests. Parties accommodate both practices well. You provide the cash by buying visitors' items. Then they spend it on her products.

It is a clever way for her to attempt entrepreneurship. She can't lose since she is guaranteed a commission from you. Plus she will profit doubly if her items sell well. Here's the caveat: if she sells costume jewelry, expect to find a lot of it in her guests' items.

Bulk Buying

The public is the successful gold buyer's main audience. Buying from the public offers the largest profit margin to you. Plus, the opportunities are plentiful. Still, you can buy from other buyers too.

Jewelers and pawnbrokers know refinery rates. However, no buyer likes waiting for refinery checks. Many jewelers and pawnbrokers enjoy unending streams of gold selling customers. They can afford to spare a few bucks in order to maintain liquidity or avoid hassle. Therefore, some of them are willing to bypass the refineries. They will accept lower rates as long as you pay cash. You will need to be well funded and equipped with a large digital scale.

Ask the buyer what his refinery pays. Then offer a little less. *This* is the time to negotiate. You are taking the risk with a small profit margin on a large cash outlay. Furthermore, unlike the general public, these guys know the math. They can make educated decisions about prices. You aim to pay as little as necessary to secure the purchase.

Each seller will agree at a different price. The price itself may vary little. Still, even small variances can balloon your bottom line. Let's say two sellers offer you 800 dwt of gold each. You can assay it for $30 per pennyweight. The first seller wants $29 per pennyweight. Thus you would earn $800 by charging him a $1 commission per pennyweight. What if the second seller agrees at $28.75 per pennyweight? That increases your commission to $1.25 per pennyweight. The extra 25¢ would profit you an additional $200 over the first seller.

It isn't feasible to lock in right after every large purchase. Instead, you must wait and combine loads before submitting them to the refinery. Your risk lurks in the waiting period. Manage your risk.

Set your current rate according to market volatility–not just current spot. Figure a margin of safety if spot price is bouncing around. Otherwise, another dip would wipe out your profit and, possibly, part of your principle. You might pay 92% on most days but only 90% on a volatile day.

Some of your business clients use refineries which don't offer lock-ins. Such clients would risk profit by mailing their assays anyway (if spot dropped during transit to the refinery). It won't surprise them that you factor volatility into your price.

Consolidate large purchases. Schedule them for same days or consecutive days. You can't buy before your sellers are ready to sell. You can't make them wait when they want to sell either. However, you can request advance notice. Coordinate the big buys in a succession that avoids idle waiting time between purchases. Then lock in as soon as you can.

Offices

Not every buyer wants to be a mobile buyer. Renting an office saves gas money and driving time. It also spares vehicle wear. *Invite* customers to your office rather than *visiting* them. That frees up more time for your other tasks. Furthermore, office rents may pleasantly surprise you. Small offices certainly cost less than storefronts.

Some companies cater specifically to budget-minded office seekers. These companies construct buildings composed entirely of small rental offices. Such offices are the entrepreneur's equivalent of an efficiency apartment.

Monthly rents in my city (in the aforementioned buildings) were around $300 for a 100-square foot, one-room office. The companies furnished each with a small table, two chairs, and a mini fridge. Offices in one building featured picture windows overlooking a fountain. It seemed perfect for a gold buyer.

These same buildings provide additional services a la carte. Internet, fax, photocopy, and answering services are typical. You can even rent a meeting room. Depending on the cost, this could be ideal for hosting gold parties. The campuses near me were upscale and impressive.

Renting an office might save you money over going mobile. Otherwise, you might just prefer it. Survey the options in your area. Calculate the cost or savings, and weigh the benefits and drawbacks.

Coins

Many coins will cross your path over time. Some of them will hold numismatic (collectible) value. Plan to profit from these items eventually. Check with your refinery as to whether they buy numismatics. Alternatively, contact a local coin dealer and discuss selling him the collectible coins you buy.

For each coin, you need to know what to pay and what to expect from your buyer. Ask your buyer to show you some basics. His guidance will help you examine and grade the coins accurately. Over time he will probably show you finer points. Once you learn enough, you can circumvent the middleman and resell coins directly to the public.

Fine Watches

Enlist a watch dealer. *Some* fine watches, like Rolexes, are worth *more* than their weight in gold. Rolexes are to standard gold watches as rare numismatics are to junk silver. Both hold commodity value; only one carries additional demand-based value.

Many factors affect a fine watch's value. You need to validate authenticity and determine condition. You also need to know if any original parts have been replaced. The list of considerations is long, as with collectible coins. Most of all you must study the science or work with a professional.

Find a good dealer and propose a deal. He'll examine fine watches for you in your customers' presence. If he wants the watch, he can discretely offer you his honest buying price. If he refuses the watch, you pay him a discounted appraisal fee.

Offer the seller a lower price than the buyer offered you. Just subtract your commission. Hopefully, your client sells you the watch and leaves. Hence you resell it to the dealer or resell it somewhere else.

EBay

A single appointment prompted Metal Man's Ebay adventure. The client met with me to sell his silver bullion stash. It totaled approximately 5-troy pounds of collector rounds, bars, and sets. Original boxes and COAs accompanied every item.

The client coolly demanded $1 under spot. That figured out to a 95% rate! My *refinery* paid 95% to me, which is why I usually paid 75–80% to clients. I couldn't meet his condition except to venture outside of my "fair pricing" policy. However, I wanted to profit from the appointment. Quickly, I considered my choices.

I knew some buyers resold bullion *above* spot prices on eBay. Metal Man had not explored that option, though; I assumed it was complicated. This situation seemed to call for it. So I took a chance in order to experiment. Eventually, I negotiated $2 under spot for the entire load.

I promptly ordered two books from Amazon about selling on eBay.[$] I read and extensively highlighted both of them within a few days. Next I set up an eBay seller account. I followed the authors' dictates; the result astounded me. From then on, Metal Man paid all clients more for bullion.

Buyers on eBay devour coins and bullion. Moreover, they pay premium prices. A well-presented auction listing will always sell above spot.

Feedback is the primary criteria by which buyers judge sellers. Hence you need adequate positive feedback. Any negative feedback will deter buyers. Unknown and negatively reviewed sellers forfeit profit.

Auction descriptions must be clear, complete, and accurate. A bent ingot is not necessarily undesirable. On the other hand, nobody wants a bent ingot that was described as being in "excellent condition".

Post good pictures and specify a return policy. Buyers rarely return bullion, but a simple return policy provides peace of mind. Learn more from leading books on the subject (Appendix C).

[$] Both books, along with many others, are available at The Gold Buyer Supplier.

Other Resale

Resale markets exist for other items besides coins and bullion. Some portion of your jewelry will be resalable too. Consider the following two proven resale strategies. Then keep your eyes open for other opportunities.

One of my fellow gold buyers opened a flea market booth. He didn't need the money but liked to try new things. Don't laugh. The booth boasted low rent, weekend only hours, and guaranteed foot traffic. It cost him little to position his business in front of crowds of people

The booth gave him storeowner status. He sold coins from his display cases at a premium there. Alongside them he presented watch parts, gemstones, and inexpensive jewelry. Of course he also bought gold there—from passersby and weekend clients whom he invited there. That tiny booth generated enviable revenue for him.

Earlier I advised you to *advertise* through free online classified ads. Well, you can *resell* on those same sites too. Two sites which hosted my "wanted" ads were popular in my area. They attracted a lot of *virtual* foot traffic. Accordingly, I regularly posted "for sale" ads on them.

Scrapping flawless necklaces and rings bothered me after a while. It seemed like such a waste . . . of money. So I created some classified ads with basic descriptions and close-up pictures. Numerous ads lack either or both of those features. Avoid that mistake.

Describe your items clearly. Many readers don't ask questions about unclear ads; they just move on. Think of what you would want to know as a potential buyer. Then address those questions. You want to hook the shopper, so include flattering photos (of the *items*).

Rings are the most profitable resale items. Most rings don't weigh much and aren't worth much as scrap. Yet they resell far above spot value—especially gemstone rings. Through resale channels, gemstone rings earned me double or triple a refinery's price. Additionally, my buyers saved money over retail prices.

You can list items for resale temporarily. Try it while accumulating enough for an assay. The items that resell will generously reward your effort. Unsold items can be scrapped as usual.

Future

Business owners must prepare for their own futures. Entrepreneurship doesn't provide a retirement plan. Fortunately, a successful gold buyer is on the inside track. Invest in gold and silver for tomorrow just as you count on them today.

Don't sell *everything* you buy. Hold back a bit of scrap from each assay. Keeping 5% of your purchases costs you nothing. You still profit handsomely from the other 95% you assay. Consequently, the withheld portion is essentially *free* to you. Consider it your own 401K (or maybe 24K) plan.

The gold you keep will be an active investment. It will accrue over time and increase in value. Some day in the future, God willing, you will have a closet full of treasure.

Then you can sell it to a refinery and retire. Otherwise, pass it on to your kids or donate it to a worthy cause.

You can also build your base with bullion. Some refineries offer alternative settlements in bullion, or money *and* bullion mixed. Why opt for a full or partial bullion payment? In doing so you are purchasing an investor commodity at wholesale prices. The bullion only costs what you paid for the scrap plus refinery fees. In a pinch, you can liquidate bullion almost instantly. Plus you can sell it at premium prices.

Your refinery may impose an additional charge for bullion payment. A small fee doesn't compromise profit much. A large fee negates the value of this option. Usually the total cost (bullion charge + assay fee + scrap purchase price) runs less than spot price. Otherwise, you can opt simply to keep the bullion you buy and only refine or resell the scrap.

Imagine this scenario as an example. You pay clients 65% of spot for gold scrap. You assay a gold load and request bullion settlement. The refinery charges a 10% commission. The result is as if you paid a 75% rate for the bullion. Normally, you pay *clients* a standard 80% rate on bullion. That means a bullion payment from the refinery (for 75%) costs less than retaining the bullion you purchase (for 80%) directly from clients.

CONCLUSION

This book represents my absolute best effort to share with you everything I know about gold buying. Many people have sought these secrets. Many people could have prospered from them. Only now are they available in a comprehensive manual. Nobody else, ever before, revealed all this information in a published book. Best of all, you found it.

As a successful gold buyer I dealt primarily with gold and silver. However, most of the information in this book translates to other precious metals. Nonetheless, you will need to learn a few more details before buying platinum, palladium, etc. Research the specifics of identification and testing if you are interested in these options.

Visit my website at *www.beagoldbuyer.com* for more resources. Browse photo galleries of coins, bullion, and gemstones. Learn more about professional associations. Additionally, visit The Gold Buyer Supplier (in the US and UK) by clicking on the links.

I don't personally sell any items. Instead, The Gold Buyer Supplier estore partners with Amazon to bring together a complete inventory of gold buyer provisions. GBS offers everything you might need, all in one place. So you can stock up on provisions while saving time and money.

I invite your emails too. You can contact me through the website. Please send your reviews and testimonials, or suggest additions or clarifications for future editions of this book. Please also consider posting your review on Amazon.

You bought this book, in part, due to my marketing statements. Please accept my humble "Thank you" for investing your money in my promise. I have worked tirelessly on this book (just ask my family) to give you the best return possible.

May God's abundant blessing meet and exceed all of your needs.

-Metal Man
Author and Former Successful Gold Buyer

APPENDIX A:

COMMON WORLD BULLION COINS

This section details *common* world bullion coins. Coins are grouped by their respective countries of origin. The available sizes (indicating precious metal content) are listed to the right of each coin. Some uncommon coins and sizes may not appear here.

Australia

Gold Lunar: 1/20, 1/10, 1/4, 1/2, 1, 2, and 10 ozt, 1/2, 1, and 10 kg
Gold Mini Roo: 0.5 g
Gold Nugget (Kangaroo): 1/20, 1/10, 1/4, 1/2, 1, and 10 ozt, 1 kg
Silver Koala: 1/2, 1, and 10 ozt, 1 kg
Silver Kookaburra: 1, 2, and 10 ozt, 1 kg
Silver Lunar: 1/2, 1, 2, 5, and 10 ozt, 1/2 and 1 kg
Platinum Koala: 1/20, 1/10, 1/4, 1/2, 1, 2, and 10 ozt, 1 kg

Austria (Vienna)

Gold Philharmonic: 1/10, 1/4, 1/2, and 1 ozt
Silver Philharmonic: 1 ozt

Britain

Gold Britannia: $\frac{1}{10}$, $\frac{1}{4}$, $\frac{1}{2}$, and 1 ozt
Gold Half Sovereign: 0.1177 ozt
Gold Sovereign: 0.2354 ozt
Silver Britannia: $\frac{1}{10}$, $\frac{1}{4}$, $\frac{1}{2}$, and 1 ozt

Canada

Gold Maple Leaf: $\frac{1}{10}$, $\frac{1}{4}$, $\frac{1}{2}$, and 1 ozt
Silver Maple Leaf: 1 ozt
Platinum Maple Leaf: $\frac{1}{20}$, $\frac{1}{10}$, $\frac{1}{4}$, $\frac{1}{2}$, and 1 ozt[$]
Palladium Maple Leaf: 1 ozt

China

Gold Panda: $\frac{1}{20}$, $\frac{1}{10}$, $\frac{1}{4}$, $\frac{1}{2}$, and 1 ozt
Silver Panda: $\frac{1}{4}$, $\frac{1}{2}$, 1, 5 and 12 ozt, 1 kg[$]
Platinum Panda: $\frac{1}{20}$, $\frac{1}{10}$, $\frac{1}{4}$, 1/2, and 1 ozt
Palladium Panda: $\frac{1}{2}$ and 1 ozt

Mexico

Gold Libertad: $\frac{1}{20}$, $\frac{1}{10}$, $\frac{1}{4}$, $\frac{1}{2}$, 1 ozt
Silver Libertad: $\frac{1}{20}$, $\frac{1}{10}$, $\frac{1}{4}$, $\frac{1}{2}$, 1, 2, and 5 ozt, 1 kg

---

[$] Canada minted a $\frac{1}{15}$ ozt Platinum Maple Leaf in 1994.
[$] Panda coins were not minted in .999 silver until 1987, and then they were limited to proofs (special coins—largely unavailable). Beginning in 1989, Silver Pandas were minted in larger quantities.

New Zealand

Gold Kiwi: ⅒, ¼, ½, and 1 ozt
Silver Fern: 1 ozt
Silver Kiwi: 1 ozt

South Africa

Gold Krugerrand: ⅒, ¼, ½, and 1 ozt

USA

Gold Buffalo: 1 ozt
Gold Eagle: ⅒, ¼, ½, and 1 ozt
Silver Eagle: 1 ozt
Platinum Eagle: ⅒, ¼, ½, and 1 ozt

APPENDIX B:

COMMON WORLD SILVER COINS

This appendix details *common* world junk silver coins, grouped by respective countries of origin. From left to right, the tables present each coin and its years of mintage. Many of the coins were produced before the years shown. Yet the earlier versions are numismatics—not junk silver. The third column shows each coin's silver composition as a percentage.

The fourth column clarifies how many of each coin comprise a whole dollar or crown. Beside this number is its decimal equivalent (in parenthesis). For instance, Table A-1 shows that there are 5 shillings per crown. Therefore, each shilling is worth .20 crown. This expression helps you count face value when dealing with unfamiliar foreign coins.

The final column presents an approximate silver content per dollar or crown.[$] You will use this to calculate BPP for the different varieties. Notes below each table offer additional points.

[$] You can calculate value per pound (£) too, but that involves converting pre-decimal to decimal values. Maybe it's because I'm American, but I find it much easier to calculate value per crown.

AUSTRALIAN SILVER COINS

Coin	Year	Percent Silver	Coins Per Crown	Silver Per Crown
Threepence	1910–1944	92.5%	20 (.05)	.84
Threepence	1947–1964	50%	20 (.05)	.454
Sixpence	1910–1945	92.5%	10 (.10)	.84
Sixpence	1946–1963	50%	10 (.10)	.454
Shilling	1910–1944	92.5%	5 (.20)	.84
Shilling	1946–1963	50%	5 (.20)	.454
Florin	1910–1945	92.5%	2.5 (.40)	.84
Florin	1946–1963	50%	2.5 (.40)	.454

Table B-1

BRITISH SILVER COINS

Coin	Year	Percent Silver	Coins Per Crown	Silver Per Crown
Threepence	1911–1919	92.5%	20 (.05)	.84
Threepence	1920–1945	50%	20 (.05)	.454
Sixpence	1911–1919	92.5%	10 (.10)	.84
Sixpence	1920–1946	50%	10 (.10)	.454
Shilling	1911–1919	92.5%	5 (.20)	.84
Shilling	1920–1946	50%	5 (.20)	.454
Florin	1911–1919	92.5%	2.5 (.40)	.84
Florin	1920–1946	50%	2.5 (.40)	.454
Half Crown	1911–1919	92.5%	2 (.50)	.84
Half Crown	1920–1946	50%	2 (.50)	.454
Crown	1927–1937	50%	1	.454

Table B-2

🗁 Britain also minted nickel-brass three pence (1937–1945). Only the silver version bears Saint George's shield on the reverse side.

🗁 1£ of 92.5% coins contains 3.3 ozt of silver

🗁 1£ of 50% coins contains 1.8 ozt of silver

CANADIAN SILVER COINS

Coin	Year	Percent Silver	Coins Per Dollar	Silver Per Dollar
Dime	1920–1966	80%	10 (.10)	.60
Dime	1967	80% or 50%	10 (.10)	.60 or .375
Dime	1968	50% or non-silver	10 (.10)	.375 or 0
Quarter	1920–1966	90%	4 (.25)	.60
Quarter	1967	80% or 50%	4 (.25)	.60 or .375
Quarter	1968	50% or non-silver	4 (.25)	.375 or 0
Half Dollar	1920–1966	80%	2 (.50)	.60
Dollar	1920–1966	80%	1	.60

Table B-3

- Canada minted two 80% and 50% dimes and quarters simultaneously (1967). You must assume 50% silver content for these.

- Canada minted 50% silver and non-silver dimes and quarters simultaneously (1968). The non-silver coins are magnetic.

NEW ZEALAND SILVER COINS

Coin	Year	Percent Silver	Coins Per Crown	Silver Per Crown
Threepence	1930–1946	50%	20 (.05)	.454
Sixpence	1933–1946	50%	10 (.10)	.454
Shilling	1933–1946	50%	5 (.20)	.454
Florin	1933–1946	50%	2.5 (.40)	.454
Half Crown	1933–1935, 1940	50%	2 (.50)	.454
Crown	1935	50%	1	.454

Table B-4

US Silver Coins

Coin	Year	Percent Silver	Coins Per Dollar	Silver Per Dollar
Nickel	1942–1945	35% or 0	20 (.05)	1.125
Dime	1916–1964	90%	10 (.10)	.725
Quarter	1932–1964	90%	4 (.25)	.725
Half Dollar	1916–1964	90%	2 (.50)	.725
Half Dollar	1965–1970	40%	2 (.50)	.296
Dollar	1878–1935	90%	1	.725

Table B-5

- Silver nickels are called “War Nickels”, and only those with mint marks (S, D, and P) on the reverse (tail) side contain silver.

- The 40% half dollars are called “silver-clad”.

- $1.40 of 90% fractional silver (not dollar coins) holds 1 ozt silver content.

APPENDIX C:

RESOURCES

Neither the author nor the publisher receives financial compensation for the following recommendations. Rather, think of this list as Metal Man's rolodex. I personally used all of these resources except the associations and some of the refineries. However, I listed every good option that I could find in order to provide every buyer with plenty of choices.

Associations

British Jewellers' Association
http://bja.org.uk

Canadian Gemmological Association
www.canadiangemmological.com

Gemmological Association
www.gem.org.au (AU)
www.gemmology.org.nz (NZ)
www.gem-a.com (UK)

Gemological Institute of America
www.gia.edu

Jewellers Association of Australia
www.jaa.com.au

Jewelers Ethics Association (USA)
www.jewelersethicsassociation.com

Jewelers of America (USA)
www.jewelers.org

National Pawnbrokers Association (USA)
www.nationalpawnbrokers.org

National Pawnbrokers Association of the UK, The
www.thenpa.com

Books

eBay 101
By Steve Weber

Guerilla Marketing
By Jay Conrad Levinson

Guerilla Publicity
By Jay Conrad Levinson, Rick Frishman, and Jill Lubin

Powerseller Secrets
By Debra Schepp and Brad Schepp

COMEX Information

USA Gold
www.usagold.com

Marketing Materials

Branders
1.877.292.4891
www.branders.com

Vistaprint
www.vistaprint.com

Navigation

Google Maps
www.maps.google.com

MapQuest
www.mapquest.com

Refineries

Albar Precious Metal Refining
Pompano Beach, Florida, USA
1.800.241.1811
www.albarmetals.com

Almanon, Inc.
Santa Ana, California, USA
1.800.626.6630
www.almanon.com

CNC Gold Refining, Inc.
Toronto, Ontario, Canada
1.416.642.3600
1.877.GOLD497
www.goldrefining.ca

D-MMEX Easy Refine
Canada, UK, USA, and
Auckland, New Zealand
1.519.255.0156 (Canada)
1.877.255.0156 (Canada)
44.20.8357.0357 (UK)
1.800.741.3174 (USA)
1.800.860.2272, ext. 465 (USA)
www.easyrefine.co.uk

G&S Metals
Ann Arbor, Michigan, USA
1.734.662.9344
1.800.852.3860
www.gsgold.com

Garfield Refining Company
Philadelphia, Pennsylvania, USA
1.215.743.4653
1.800.523.0968
www.garfieldrefining.com

Gold Bullion Australia
Brisbane, Melbourne, Sydney, and Gold Coast, Australia
1.300.754.602 (Head Office—Gold Coast)
617.5538.9200 (Intl.)
www.goldbullionaustralia.com.au

Imperial Smelting & Refining Co.
Markham, Ontario, Canada
Warwick, Rhode Island, USA
1.800.263.1669, ext. 2902 (Canada)
www.imperialproducts.com

Kitco Inc.
Montreal, Quebec, Canada
Rouses Point, New York, USA
1.514.875.4820 (Canada)
1.866.925.4826 (US)
www.kitco.com/jewelry

London Refinery, The
London, England
California, USA
www.thelondonrefinery.com

Midwest Refineries
Waterford, Michigan, USA
1.800.356.2955
www.midwestrefineries.com

Northeastern Metal Corp.
Stamford, Connecticut, USA
1.203.348.8088
1.800.243.2452

Plus Gold
Birmingham, England
0121 236 7597
www.plusgold.com

RMC²
Miami, Florida, USA
1.305.685.8505
1.888.685.8505
www.rmcsquared.com

Silvertowne
Winchester, Indiana, USA
1.800.788.7481
www.silvertowne.com

WEB HOSTING

Go Daddy
1.480.505.8877
www.godaddy.com

OTHER

Panda Collector[$]
www.pandacollector.com/rogue

[$] This site offers a section to help you identify phony Chinese Panda coins.

INDEX

You may wonder about the conspicuous absence of "gold", "silver" and "gold buyer" from this index. These terms are mentioned hundreds of times throughout this book. Thus their inclusion would add frivolous pages to this index. I assume that, by now, you completely understand these concepts.

You will not find here specific units of measurement, markings, or coins either. I have painstakingly elaborated upon each subject it its dedicated section. Table 9.1, on page 113, explains units of measurement. See Chapter 7, starting on page 81, to study all about markings. The tables in Appendices B and C detail various common world coins.

A

B

C

D

E

F

G

O

P

R

S

T

U

V

W

CPSIA information can be obtained at www.ICGtesting.com
Printed in the USA
BVOW08s1011241213

340020BV00001B/160/P

9 780615 456089